Busy Ant Maths

2nd EDITION

Textbook 6

T0312334

Series editor and author: Peter Clarke

William Collins' dream of knowledge for all began with the publication of his first book in 1819.

A self-educated mill worker, he not only enriched millions of lives, but also founded a flourishing publishing house. Today, staying true to this spirit, Collins books are packed with inspiration, innovation and practical expertise.

They place you at the centre of a world of possibility and give you exactly what you need to explore it.

Collins. Freedom to teach.

Published by Collins

An imprint of HarperCollins*Publishers*
The News Building, 1 London Bridge Street, London,
SE1 9GF, UK

HarperCollins*Publishers*
Macken House, 39/40 Mayor Street Upper, Dublin 1,
D01 C9W8, Ireland

> Browse the complete Collins catalogue at
> **collins.co.uk**

British Library Cataloguing-in-Publication Data

A catalogue record for this publication is available from the British Library.

Series editor: Peter Clarke
Author: Peter Clarke
Product manager: Holly Woolnough
Editorial assistant: Nalisha Vansia
Copy editor: Tanya Solomons
Proofreader: Catherine Dakin
Illustrator: Ann Paganuzzi
Cover designer: Amparo Barrera
Cover illustrator: Amparo Barrera
Internal designer: 2Hoots Publishing Services
Typesetter: David Jimenez
Production controller: Alhady Ali
Printed and bound in Great Britain by Martins the Printers

> Busy Ant Maths 2nd edition components are compatible with the 1st edition of Busy Ant Maths.

MIX
Paper | Supporting
responsible forestry
FSC™ C007454

This book contains FSC™ certified paper and other controlled sources to ensure responsible forest management.

For more information visit: www.harpercollins.co.uk/green

Contents

Fractions

Decimals

Percentages

Year 6 Number facts

How to use this book

This book shows different pictures, models and images (representations) to explain important mathematical ideas to do with number.

The key words related to the mathematical ideas are shown in **colour**. It's important that you understand what each of these words mean.

At the start of each double page is a brief description of the key mathematical ideas.

The main part of each double page explains the mathematical ideas. It might include pictures, models or an example.

Your teacher will talk to you about the images on the pages.

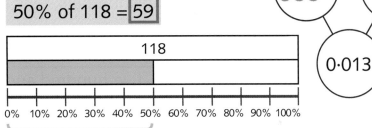

100,000s	10,000s	1,000s	100s	10s	1s
3	7	4	8	5	1

50% of 118 = 59

118

0% 10% 20% 30% 40% 50% 60% 70% 80% 90% 100%

? — 118 ÷ 2 = 59

0·013

Sometimes there might be questions to think about or an activity to do.

 Say

 Build

 Draw

 Write

Pages 6-7

This refers to mathematical ideas on other pages that you need to understand before learning about the ideas on these two pages.

Pages 24-29, 48-55

This refers to mathematical ideas on other pages that use or build upon the ideas on these two pages.

 This helps you think more deeply about the mathematical ideas.

 Hint Use the pages in this book to help you answer the questions in the Pupil Books.

Numbers to 10,000,000

The place of each digit in a number tells us its value. Composing and decomposing numbers make them easier to calculate.

5-digit numbers

5-digit numbers are made of **tens of thousands** (10,000s), thousands (1,000s), **hundreds** (100s), tens (10s) and ones (1s).

94,586 is a 5-digit number.

10,000s	1,000s	100s	10s	1s
9	4	5	8	6

To find the whole number, we add the values together.

90,000 + 4,000 + 500 + 80 + 6 = 94,586

5-digit numbers have two thousands numbers: **tens of thousands** (10,000s) and thousands (1,000s).

So, 94,586 has 94 thousands, 5 **hundreds**, 8 tens and 6 ones.

We say: ninety-four thousand, five hundred and eighty-six

6-digit numbers

6-digit numbers are made of **hundreds of thousands** (100,000s), **tens of thousands** (10,000s), thousands (1,000s), **hundreds** (100s), tens (10s) and ones (1s).

374,851 is a 6-digit number.

100,000s	10,000s	1,000s	100s	10s	1s
3	7	4	8	5	1

To find the whole number, we add the values together.

300,000 + 70,000 + 4,000 + 800 + 50 + 1 = 374,851

6-digit numbers have three thousands numbers: **hundreds of thousands** (100,000s), **tens of thousands** (10,000s) and thousands (1,000s).

So, 374,851 has 374 thousands, 8 **hundreds**, 5 tens and 1 one.

We say: three hundred and seventy-four thousand, eight hundred and fifty-one

4-, 5- and 6-digit numbers can be written with a comma or a space separating the **hundreds** and the thousands.

7,568, 94,586 and 374,851
or
7 568, 94 586 and 374 851

Millions

7-digit numbers are made of **millions** (1,000,000), **hundreds of thousands** (100,000s), **tens of thousands** (10,000s), thousands (1,000s), **hundreds** (100s), tens (10s) and ones (1s).

2,546,389 is a 7-digit number.

1,000,000s	100,000s	10,000s	1,000s	100s	10s	1s
2	5	4	6	3	8	9

To find the whole number, we add the values together.
2,000,000 + 500,000 + 40,000 + 6,000 + 300 + 80 + 9 = 2,546,389

We say: two million, five hundred and forty-six thousand, three hundred and eighty-nine

7-digit numbers can be written with a comma or a space separating the **hundreds** and the thousands, and the **hundreds of thousands** and the **millions**.

2,546,389
or
2546389

We can represent 7-digit numbers with a part-whole model showing the **millions** and thousands, and the **hundreds**, tens and ones.

2,546,389

thousands

hundreds, tens and ones

millions

2,000,000   546,000   389

Look at the Gattegno chart below. It shows **millions, hundreds of thousands, tens of thousands,** thousands, **hundreds,** tens and ones.

What patterns do you notice? How are the rows the same? How are they different? What happens in each column of numbers?

Say

Point to numbers in different rows and say the number name.

1,000,000	2,000,000	3,000,000	4,000,000	5,000,000	6,000,000	7,000,000	8,000,000	9,000,000
100,000	200,000	300,000	400,000	500,000	600,000	700,000	800,000	900,000
10,000	20,000	30,000	40,000	50,000	60,000	70,000	80,000	90,000
1,000	2,000	3,000	4,000	5,000	6,000	7,000	8,000	9,000
100	200	300	400	500	600	700	800	900
10	20	30	40	50	60	70	80	90
1	2	3	4	5	6	7	8	9

Pages 8-37

Represent numbers to 10,000,000 in different ways

Pages 6-7

We can decompose numbers to show the place value of each digit. We can also decompose (or regroup) numbers in other ways.

4-digit numbers

We can **decompose** or **partition** 8,374 into thousands, **hundreds**, tens and ones.

We can decompose or **regroup** 8,374 in other ways to help with calculations.

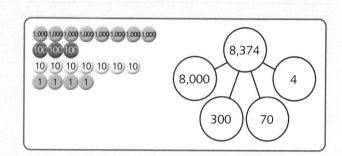

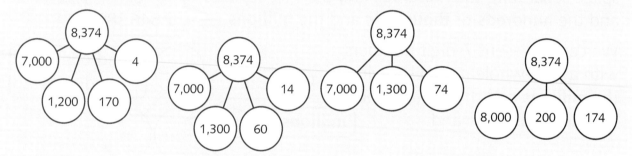

5-digit numbers

We can decompose or partition 39,216 into tens of thousands, thousands, **hundreds**, tens and ones.

We can decompose or regroup 39,216 in other ways.

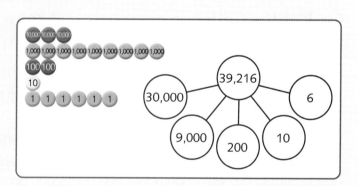

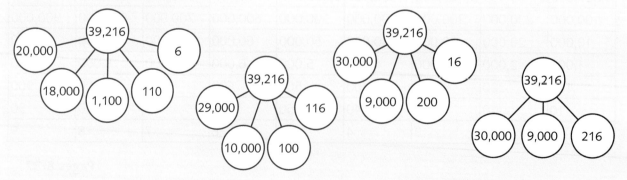

6-digit numbers

We can decompose or partition 537,482 into **hundreds of thousands**, **tens of thousands**, thousands, **hundreds**, tens and ones.

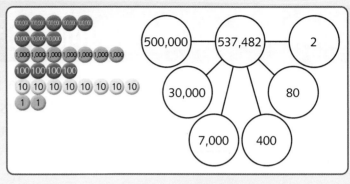

We can decompose or regroup 537,482 in other ways.

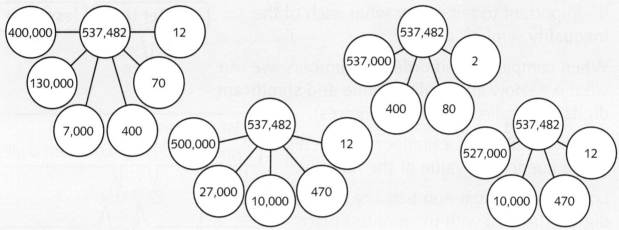

7-digit numbers

We can decompose or partition 3,164,275 into **millions**, **hundreds of thousands**, **tens of thousands**, thousands, **hundreds**, tens and ones.

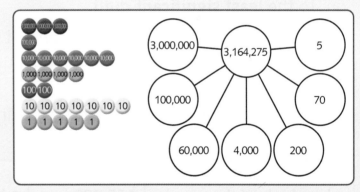

We can decompose or regroup 3,164,275 in other ways.

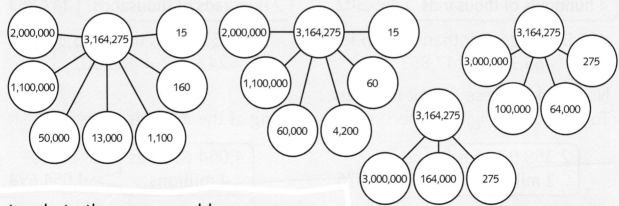

In what other ways could you regroup each of the numbers on pages 8 and 9?

Pages 18-23, 30-37

Compare and order numbers to 10,000,000

Pages 6-7

We can compare and order numbers with the same number of digits, and with different numbers of digits, using our knowledge of place value. We can also use the inequality symbols, < and >, to compare and order numbers.

It's important to remember what each of the inequality symbols mean.

greater than   **less than**

When **comparing** and **ordering** numbers, we use what we know about **place value** and **significant digits** (also called **significant figures**).

>   <

Significant digits of a number are the digits that influence the **value** of the number.

| 1st (or most) significant digit | 3rd significant digit |

Look at this 4-digit number. The **most significant digit** is the digit with the greatest place value, the next digit is the second, and so on, to the **least significant digit**.

2 7 0 9

| 2nd significant digit | 4th (or least) significant digit |

When comparing and ordering numbers, it's important to start with the digits with the greatest place value – the most significant digits.

Look at these 6-digit numbers.
To **compare** 6-digit numbers, start by looking at the **hundreds of thousands** digits.

465,302 has
4 hundreds of thousands. **4**65,302

247,853 has
2 hundreds of thousands. **2**47,853

465,302 is greater than 247,853.
465,302 > 247,853

247,853 is less than 465,302.
247,853 < 465,302

Now look at these 7-digit numbers.
To compare 7-digit numbers, start by looking at the **millions** digits.

2,358,576 has
2 millions. **2,358,576**

4,054,698 has
4 millions. **4,054,698**

2,358,576 is less than 4,054,698.
2,358,576 < 4,054,698

4,054,698 is greater than 2,358,576.
4,054,698 > 2,358,576

If the digits of the most significant digits are the same, we look at the place value columns to the right until they are different digits.

Now look at these two 7-digit numbers.
The **millions** and **hundreds of thousands** digits are the same, so look at the **tens of thousands** digits – the 3rd most significant digits.

| 6,842,481 has 4 tens of thousands. | 6,8**4**2,481 |

| 6,891,423 has 9 tens of thousands. | 6,8**9**1,423 |

6,842,481 is less than 6,891,423.
6,842,481 < 6,891,423

6,891,423 is greater than 6,842,481.
6,891,423 > 6,842,481

We can **order** a set of numbers:

in **ascending** order – from **smallest** to **largest/greatest**

or in **descending** order – from largest/greatest to smallest.

Look at these numbers.

1,000,000s	100,000s	10,000s	1,000s	100s	10s	1s
		6	5	3	1	0
	3	1	0	4	2	8
			9	9	6	7
1	0	0	4	2	3	6
	3	1	0	2	2	8
		6	5	3	0	4

What's the same about the numbers? What's different?

When comparing and ordering numbers with the same number of digits, if their most significant digits are equal in value, what do you look at next?

What's different about comparing and ordering numbers with the same number of digits and comparing and ordering numbers with different numbers of digits?

Place this set of numbers in ascending order.

| 652,109 | 99,999 | 1,043,278 |

| 652,019 | 1,304,278 | 900,002 |

Pages 62-63

Round numbers to 10,000,000

Pages 6-7

Rounding means changing a number to another number that is close to it in value, which may make the number easier to use. Rounding is a useful strategy to use when estimating.

Round to the nearest 10

When **rounding** numbers to the nearest **multiple of 10**, look at the ones digit to decide whether to **round up** to the **next** multiple of 10 or **round down** to the **previous** multiple of 10.

We can round 2-, 3-, 4-, 5-, 6- and 7-digit numbers to the nearest 10.

78 is closer to 80 than to 70. So, round up to the next multiple of 10, which is 80.

73 is closer to 70 than to 80. So, round down to the previous multiple of 10, which is 70.

75 is exactly **halfway between** 70 and 80. So, round up to the next multiple of 10.

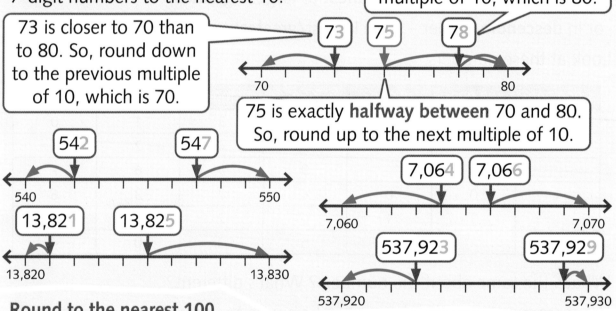

Round to the nearest 100

When rounding to the nearest **multiple of 100**, look at the tens digit to decide whether to round up to the next multiple of 100 or round down to the previous multiple of 100.

We can round 3-, 4-, 5-, 6- and 7-digit numbers to the nearest 100.

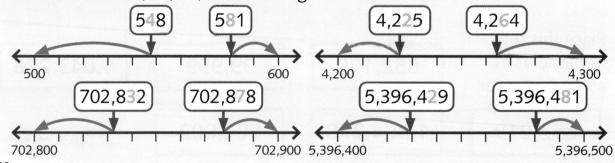

Round to the nearest 1,000

When rounding to the nearest **multiple of 1,000**, look at the **hundreds** digit to decide whether to round up to the next multiple of 1,000 or round down to the previous multiple of 1,000.

We can round 4-, 5-, 6- and 7-digit numbers to the nearest 1,000.

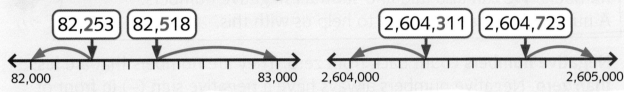

Round to the nearest 10,000

When rounding to the nearest **multiple of 10,000**, look at the thousands digit to decide whether to round up to the next multiple of 10,000 or round down to the previous multiple of 10,000.

We can round 5-, 6- and 7-digit numbers to the nearest 10,000.

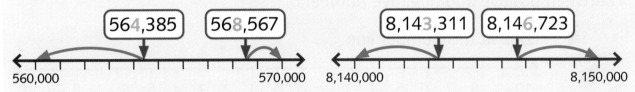

Round to the nearest 100,000

When rounding to the nearest **multiple of 100,000**, look at the tens of thousands digit to decide whether to round up to the next multiple of 100,000 or round down to the previous multiple of 100,000.

We can round 6- and 7-digit numbers to the nearest 100,000.

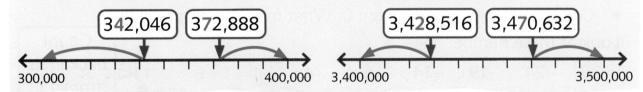

Round to the nearest 1,000,000

When rounding to the nearest **multiple of 1,000,000**, look at the hundreds of thousands digit to decide whether to round up to the next multiple of 1,000,000 or round down to the previous multiple of 1,000,000.

We can round 7-digit numbers to the nearest 1,000,000.

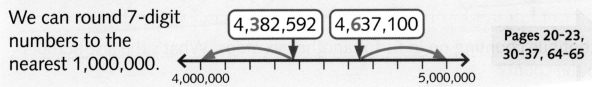

Pages 20-23, 30-37, 64-65

Negative numbers

Just like positive numbers, we can count on and back in negative numbers. We can also add and subtract negative numbers.
A number line is a useful tool to help us with this.

Negative numbers count back from zero. They are numbers that are **less than zero**. Negative numbers always have a negative sign (–) in front of them, such as –4.

We say: ⟨ negative four ⟩

Positive numbers count on from zero. They are numbers that are **greater than** zero.

Zero is neither a positive nor a negative number. It's the separation point between positive and negative numbers.

 Say Look at this number line.

←————————————————————————————→
–10 –9 –8 –7 –6 –5 –4 –3 –2 –1 0 1 2 3 4 5 6 7 8 9 10

- Start on 10 and count back 12. What number do you land on?
- Start on –10 and count on 16. What number do you land on?
- Count on in steps of 10 from 0. What is the 6th step?
- Count back in steps of 10 from 0. What must the 6th step be?
- Count on in steps of 8 from 0. What is the 8th step?
- Count back in steps of 8 from 0. What must the 8th step be?

Look at these number lines.

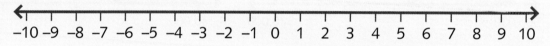

-29   -24   -19   -14   -9   -4   1   6   11 ⟨ Count back in 5s from 11.

Count on in 6s from -25.

Continue counting back in 5s for another six steps. What's the last number in the count?

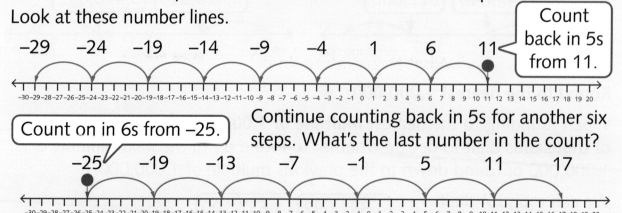

-25   -19   -13   -7   -1   5   11   17

Continue counting on in 6s for another six steps. What's the last number in the count?

We can use a number line to help us add and subtract positive and negative numbers.

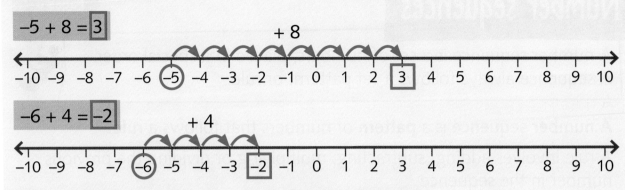

$-5 + 8 = 3$

$+8$

$-6 + 4 = -2$

$+4$

We can think of subtraction as finding the **difference**.

The difference between 3 and –6 is 9.

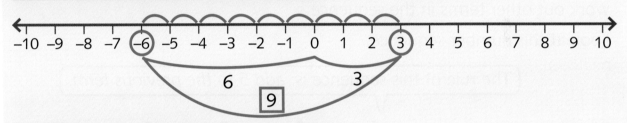

6

3

9

The difference between –5 and 8 is 13.

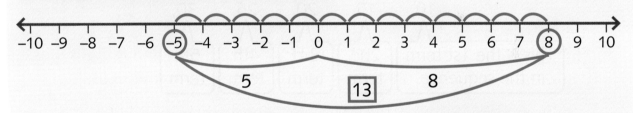

5

13

8

We can also use a number scale, such as **temperatures** on a **thermometer**, to add and subtract negative numbers.

°C

What temperature does the thermometer show?

If the temperature drops by 1 °C, what temperature will the thermometer show?

If the temperature increases by 6 °C, what temperature will the thermometer show?

If, in 6 hours' time, the temperature shows 4 °C, by how much has the temperature increased?

Number sequences

Pages 6-7

A number sequence is a set of numbers, placed in a special order.
A sequence always follows a set pattern, or rule.

A **number sequence** is a **pattern** of numbers that follows a **rule**.

A rule involves adding, subtracting, multiplying or dividing the previous number in the sequence.

The numbers in a sequence are called **terms**.

When we know the rule for a number sequence, we can apply the rule to work out other terms in the sequence.

Look at this number sequence.

The rule of this sequence is: *add 5 to the previous term.*

+ 5   + 5   + 5   + 5

10,   15,   20,   25,   30,   …

This is the 1st term in the sequence.   2nd term   3rd term   4th term   5th term

What are the next three terms in the sequence?

The rule of this sequence is: *subtract 8 from the previous term.*

− 8   − 8   − 8   − 8   − 8

91,   83,   75,   67,   59,   51,   …

What are the next three terms in the sequence?

Write Work out the rule for each of these sequences. Then apply the rule to work out the next three terms in each sequence.

17, 28, 39, 50, 61, …   20, 14, 8, 2, −4, …

234, 214, 194, 174, …

In this number sequence, the rule involves multiplication.

The rule of this sequence is: *multiply the previous term by 10.*

× 10   × 10   × 10   × 10

1,   10,   100,   1,000, 10,000,   ...

Look at this number sequence.

The rule of this sequence is: *multiply the previous term by 3.*

× 3   × 3   × 3

1,   3,   9,   27,   ...

What are the next two terms in the sequence?

Sometimes, we need to work out terms that come before the given terms in a sequence.
Look at this number sequence.

The rule of this sequence is: *add 3 to the previous term.*

+ 3   + 3   + 3   + 3   + 3

☐, 19,   22,   25,   28,   31,   ☐

To work out this term, we apply the rule of *add 3*. So, the **unknown term** is 34. (31 + 3)

− 3

To work out this term, we use the **inverse operation**. So, the unknown term is 16. (19 − 3)

 Write   Work out the rule for each of these sequences. Then apply the rule to work out the missing terms.

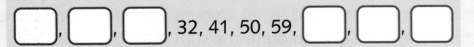
☐, ☐, ☐, 32, 41, 50, 59, ☐, ☐, ☐

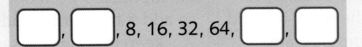
☐, ☐, 8, 16, 32, 64, ☐, ☐

☐, ☐, ☐, 50, 43, 36, 29, ☐, ☐, ☐

Mental addition and subtraction

Pages 6-9

We can use known number facts, the inverse relationship between addition and subtraction, properties of arithmetic, and place value knowledge to solve calculations mentally.

$5 + 7 = \boxed{12}$ — sum or total

addend   addend

The first addend can also be referred to as the augend.

$12 - 5 = \boxed{7}$ — difference

minuend   subtrahend

Addition and subtraction are related – they are inverse operations. That means they are opposite operations – addition reverses subtraction, and subtraction reverses addition.

We can use the following properties of arithmetic to help solve calculations mentally:

- commutative property – changing the order of the addends does not change the sum. $\quad 5 + 7 = 7 + 5$

- associative property – changing the grouping of the addends does not change the sum. $\quad 4 + 5 + 6 = 6 + 4 + 5$

Understanding and applying compensation strategies can also help us solve calculations mentally.

Compensation strategies involve looking for an easier calculation than the one you need to solve. This could be using a known fact to calculate the answer to an unknown fact, or replacing a number in the calculation with an easier number close to it, and then compensating for this later.

- If one addend is increased by an amount and the other addend is decreased by the same amount, the sum stays the same.

2 is added to one addend, so subtract 2 from the other addend to keep the sum the same.	5 is subtracted from one addend, so add 5 to the other addend to keep the sum the same.

$78 + 46 = \boxed{124}$

$+2 \downarrow \qquad \downarrow -2 \qquad =$

$80 + 44 = \boxed{124}$

$325 + 247 = \boxed{572}$

$-5 \downarrow \qquad \downarrow +5 \qquad =$

$320 + 252 = \boxed{572}$

- If the minuend and subtrahend are increased (or decreased) by the same amount, the difference stays the same.

> 2 is added to the subtrahend, so add 2 to the minuend to keep the difference the same.

> 3 is subtracted from the minuend, so subtract 3 from the subtrahend to keep the difference the same.

$$343 - 228 = \boxed{115}$$
$$+2 \downarrow \qquad \downarrow +2 \qquad \Big\} =$$
$$345 - 230 = \boxed{115}$$

$$543 - 507 = \boxed{36}$$
$$-3 \downarrow \qquad \downarrow -3 \qquad \Big\} =$$
$$540 - 504 = \boxed{36}$$

These strategies use inverse operations to calculate the answer.

- If one addend is increased (or decreased) and the other addend is kept the same, the sum increases (or decreases) by the same amount.

> 6 is added to one addend so the sum increases by 6. Subtract 6 to calculate the answer.

> 4 is subtracted from one addend so the sum decreases by 4. Add 4 to calculate the answer.

$$174 + 217 = \boxed{391}$$
$$+6 \downarrow \qquad +6 \downarrow \quad \Big) -6 =$$
$$180 + 217 = \boxed{397}$$

$$567 + 234 = \boxed{801}$$
$$-4 \downarrow \quad -4 \downarrow \quad \Big) +4 =$$
$$567 + 230 = \boxed{797}$$

- If the minuend is increased (or decreased) and the subtrahend is kept the same, the difference increases (or decreases) by the same amount.

> 3 is added to the minuend so the difference increases by 3. Subtract 3 to calculate the answer.

> 4 is subtracted from the minuend so the difference decreases by 4. Add 4 to calculate the answer.

$$172 - 35 = \boxed{137}$$
$$+3 \downarrow \qquad +3 \downarrow \quad \Big) -3 =$$
$$175 - 35 = \boxed{140}$$

$$282 - 138 = \boxed{144}$$
$$-4 \downarrow \qquad -4 \downarrow \quad \Big) +4 =$$
$$278 - 138 = \boxed{140}$$

- If the minuend is kept the same and the subtrahend is increased (or decreased), the difference decreases (or increases) by the same amount.

> 2 is added to the subtrahend so the difference decreases by 2. Add 2 to calculate the answer.

> 3 is subtracted from the subtrahend so the difference increases by 3. Subtract 3 to calculate the answer.

$$342 - 78 = \boxed{264}$$
$$+2 \downarrow \quad -2 \downarrow \quad \Big) +2 =$$
$$342 - 80 = \boxed{262}$$

$$245 - 168 = \boxed{77}$$
$$-3 \downarrow \quad +3 \downarrow \quad \Big) -3 =$$
$$245 - 165 = \boxed{80}$$

Pages 20-23, 66-67, 70-71

Add whole numbers with more than 4 digits

Pages 6-9, 12-13, 18-19

Adding numbers, such as 275,316 + 150,837 or 1,736,465 + 49,145 + 8,293, involves using knowledge of place value and recalling addition facts to 20.

$$275{,}316 + 150{,}837 = \boxed{426{,}153}$$

⚠ **ALWAYS:**
Estimate
Calculate
Check

First **partition** both numbers into **hundreds of thousands**, **tens of thousands**, thousands, **hundreds**, tens and ones.

Then add the ones. As there are more than 10 ones, we need to regroup 10 ones into 1 ten.

100,000s	10,000s	1,000s	100s	10s	1s

Next add the **hundreds of thousands**.

Then add the thousands.

Next add the tens.

Now add the **hundreds**. As there are more than 10 **hundreds**, we need to regroup 10 **hundreds** into 1 thousand.

Now add the **tens of thousands**. As there are more than 10 **tens of thousands**, we need to regroup 10 **tens of thousands** into 1 **hundred thousand**.

Finally combine the **hundreds of thousands**, tens of thousands, thousands, **hundreds**, tens and ones.

We can record this in columns.

```
      2 7 5 3 1 6
    + 1 5 0 8 3 7
              1 3
              4 0
          1 1 0 0
          5 0 0 0
      1 2 0 0 0 0
      3 0 0 0 0 0
      4 2 6 1 5 3
```

leads to

```
      2 7 5 3 1 6
    + 1 5 0 8 3 7
      4 2 6 1 5 3
        1     1     1
```

$1{,}736{,}465 + 49{,}145 + 8{,}293 = \boxed{1{,}793{,}903}$

First partition all three numbers into **millions**, **hundreds of thousands**, tens of thousands, thousands, **hundreds**, tens and ones.

Then add the ones. As there are more than 10 ones, we need to regroup 10 ones into 1 ten.

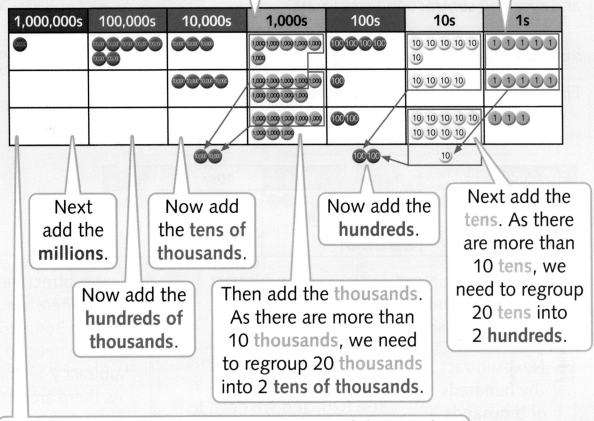

Next add the **millions**.

Now add the **tens of thousands**.

Now add the **hundreds**.

Next add the tens. As there are more than 10 tens, we need to regroup 20 tens into 2 **hundreds**.

Now add the **hundreds of thousands**.

Then add the thousands. As there are more than 10 thousands, we need to regroup 20 thousands into 2 **tens of thousands**.

Finally combine the **millions**, **hundreds of thousands**, tens of thousands, thousands, **hundreds**, tens and ones.

We can record this in columns.

```
  1 7 3 6 4 6 5
      4 9 1 4 5
+       8 2 9 3
            1 3
          1 9 0
          7 0 0
        2 3 0 0 0
        7 0 0 0 0
      7 0 0 0 0 0
    1 0 0 0 0 0 0
    1 7 9 3 9 0 3
            1
```

leads to

```
  1 7 3 6 4 6 5
      4 9 1 4 5
+       8 2 9 3
  1 7 9 3 9 0 3
        2   2 1
```

Pages 70-73

Subtract whole numbers with more than 4 digits

Pages 6–9, 12–13, 18–19

Subtracting numbers, such as 364,825 – 126,473 or 3,472,183 – 731,926, involves using knowledge of place value and recalling subtraction facts to 20.

364,825 – 126,473 = 238,352

⚠ **ALWAYS:**
Estimate
Calculate
Check

First partition 364,825 into **hundreds of thousands**, **tens of thousands**, thousands, **hundreds**, tens and ones.

Then subtract the ones.

100,000s	10,000s	1,000s	100s	10s	1s

Now subtract the **tens of thousands**.

Now subtract the **hundreds**.

Next subtract the tens. There are 2 tens in 364,825, and we need to subtract 7 tens. As there aren't enough tens in 364,825, exchange 1 **hundred** for 10 tens.

Next subtract the **hundreds of thousands**.

Then subtract the thousands. There are 4 thousands in 364,825, and we need to subtract 6 thousands. As there aren't enough thousands in 364,825, exchange 1 **ten thousand** for 10 thousands.

Finally place the partitioned number back together.

We can record this in columns.

	50,000	14,000	700	120		
300,000	6̶0̶,̶0̶0̶0̶	4̶,̶0̶0̶0̶	8̶0̶0̶	2̶0̶	5
– 100,000	20,000	6,000	400	70	3
200,000	30,000	8,000	300	50	2

leads to

```
    5  1  7  1
 3  6̶  4  8̶  2  5
-1  2  6  4  7  3
 2  3  8  3  5  2
```

200,000 + 30,000 + 8,000 + 300 + 50 + 2 = 238,352

You can also write the exchanged values like this.

```
    5 14  7 12
 3  6̶  4̶  8̶  2̶  5
-1  2  6  4  7  3
 2  3  8  3  5  2
```

$3,472,183 - 731,926 = \boxed{2,740,257}$

First partition 3,472,183 into **millions**, **hundreds of thousands**, **tens of thousands**, thousands, **hundreds**, tens and ones.

Then subtract the ones. There are 3 ones in 3,472,183, and we need to subtract 6 ones. As there aren't enough ones in 3,472,183, exchange 1 ten for 10 ones.

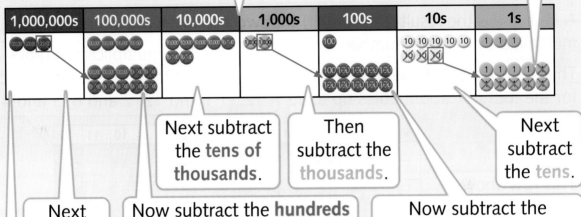

1,000,000s	100,000s	10,000s	1,000s	100s	10s	1s

Next subtract the **tens of thousands**.

Then subtract the thousands.

Next subtract the tens.

Next subtract the **millions**.

Now subtract the **hundreds of thousands**. There are 4 **hundreds of thousands** in 3,472,183, and we need to subtract 7 **hundreds of thousands**. As there aren't enough **hundreds of thousands** in 3,472,183, exchange 1 **million** for 10 **hundreds of thousands**.

Now subtract the **hundreds**. There is 1 **hundred** in 3,472,183, and we need to subtract 9 **hundreds**. As there aren't enough **hundreds** in 3,472,183, exchange 1 thousand for 10 **hundreds**.

Finally place the partitioned number back together.

We can record this in columns.

	2,000,000	1,400,000			1,000	1,100	70	13
	3,000,000	400,000	70,000	2,000	100	80	3
−		700,000	30,000	1,000	900	20	6
	2,000,000	700,000	40,000	0	200	50	7

$2,000,000 + 700,000 + 40,000 + 200 + 50 + 7 = 2,740,257$

leads to →

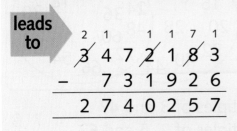

You can also write the exchanged values like this.

```
  2  14    1  11  7  13
  3  4  7  2  1  8  3
-     7  3  1  9  2  6
  2  7  4  0  2  5  7
```

Pages 70-71, 74-75

Multiples, common multiples, factors and common factors

Pages 6-7

Understanding multiples and factors helps us with multiplication and division calculations.

A **multiple** is the result (or **product**) that we get when one number is multiplied by another number.

This multiplication table shows multiples for the **multiplication tables** up to 12 × 12.

> The multiplication table shows that 12 is a multiple of: 1 and 12, 2 and 6, 3 and 4.

×	1	2	3	4	5	6	7	8	9	10	11	12
1	1	2	3	4	5	6	7	8	9	10	11	12
2	2	4	6	8	10	12	14	16	18	20	22	24
3	3	6	9	12	15	18	21	24	27	30	33	36
4	4	8	12	16	20	24	28	32	36	40	44	48
5	5	10	15	20	25	30	35	40	45	50	55	60
6	6	12	18	24	30	36	42	48	54	60	66	72
7	7	14	21	28	35	42	49	56	63	70	77	84
8	8	16	24	32	40	48	56	64	72	80	88	96
9	9	18	27	36	45	54	63	72	81	90	99	108
10	10	20	30	40	50	60	70	80	90	100	110	120
11	11	22	33	44	55	66	77	88	99	110	121	132
12	12	24	36	48	60	72	84	96	108	120	132	144

This row shows multiples of 4.

This row shows multiples of 6.

This row shows multiples of 12.

We can see from the multiplication table above that the first 12 multiples of 4 are:

4, 8, 12 , 16, 20, 24 , 28, 32, 36 , 40, 44 and 48

We can also see that the first 12 multiples of 6 are:

6, 12 , 18, 24 , 30, 36 , 42, 48 , 54, 60, 66 and 72

We can see that some numbers appear in the lists of multiples for both 4 and 6.

The multiples that are common to two or more numbers are called **common multiples**.

The first three common multiples of 4 and 6 are 12, 24 and 36.

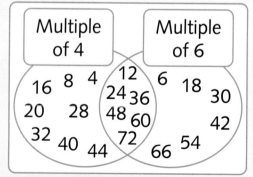

Multiple of 4 — Multiple of 6

16 8 4 12 24 36 6 18 30
20 28 48 60 42
32 40 44 72 66 54

Write
What are the first three common multiples of 3 and 4?
What are the first three common multiples of 2, 5 and 6?

Multiples are made when **factors** are multiplied together.

Factors are the **whole numbers** that we **multiply** together to get another whole number.

factor × factor = multiple

3 is a factor of 12.

4 is a factor of 12.

3 × 4 = 12

12 is a multiple of 3 and 4.

A **factor pair** is a set of two factors. When multiplied together, they make a particular product.

Every whole number has at least one factor pair – the number 1 and itself.

Let's look at these arrays and multiplication calculations for the number 12.

1 × 12 = 12

2 × 6 = 12

3 × 4 = 12

We can see from the arrays that 12 has three factor pairs. It has six factors altogether.

1 × 12 = 12   2 × 6 = 12   3 × 4 = 12

So, the factors of 12 are 1, 2, 3, 4, 6 and 12.

We can also think of a factor as a whole number that **divides exactly into** another number.

multiple ÷ factor = factor

4 is a factor of 12.

12 is a multiple of 3 and 4.

12 ÷ 4 = 3

3 is a factor of 12.

Common factors are factors that are shared by two or more numbers.

We know that the factors of 12 are 1, 2, 3, 4, 6 and 12.
The factors of 16 are 1, 2, 4, 8 and 16.
So, 1, 2 and 4 are common factors of 12 and 16.

We can see from this **Venn diagram** that the **highest common factor** (**HCF**) of 12 and 16 is 4.

Factor of 12

3   6   12   1   4
                  2

Factor of 16

8   16

Write

What are the common factors of 24 and 30?

What are the common factors of 40 and 64?

Pages 26–37, 40–43, 46–51, 86–87

Tests of divisibility

Pages 6–7, 24–25

Recognising patterns in multiplication tables, or applying a test of divisibility, can tell us whether a number can be divided exactly by a whole number without a remainder.

Divisible by means that when we **divide** one number by another number, the result (or **quotient**) is a **whole number**. In other words, 'divisible by' means 'can be **exactly divided by**'.

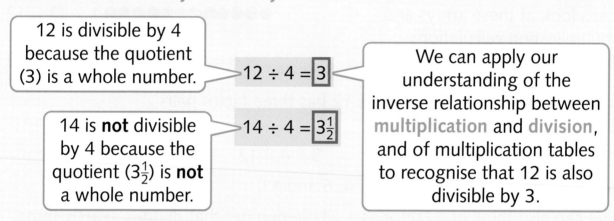

12 is divisible by 4 because the quotient (3) is a whole number.

$12 \div 4 = \boxed{3}$

We can apply our understanding of the inverse relationship between **multiplication** and **division**, and of multiplication tables to recognise that 12 is also divisible by 3.

14 is **not** divisible by 4 because the quotient ($3\frac{1}{2}$) is **not** a whole number.

$14 \div 4 = \boxed{3\frac{1}{2}}$

So, a number that is divisible by another number must also be a **multiple** of that number: 12 is a multiple of 4 (and also of 3).

We can apply **tests of divisibility** to see whether one number is a multiple of another.

The tests of divisibility for 2, 5 and 10 are very simple. They involve looking at the **ones digit** of a number.

Divisible by	Divisibility rule	Examples
2	If the ones digit is even (0, 2, 4, 6 or 8), the number is divisible by 2.	16, 194, 5,038, 70,000, 841,592, 1,302,864
5	If the ones digit is 0 or 5, the number is divisible by 5.	10, 345, 6,030, 64,295, 149,400, 5,385,835
10	If the ones digit is 0, the number is divisible by 10.	140, 4,300, 23,870, 654,380, 8,307,760

We can see from the tests of divisibility above that all the multiples of 10, 100, 1,000, 10,000, 100,000 and 1,000,000 are divisible by 2, 5 and 10.

Look at these tests of divisibility for the numbers 3, 4, 6, 8, 9 and 12.

Divisible by	Divisibility rule	Examples ✓ is divisible ✗ is not divisible
3	If the **sum of all its digits** is a multiple of 3, the number is divisible by 3.	1,224 ✓ $1 + 2 + 2 + 4 = 9$ $(9 \div 3 = 3)$ 341 ✗ $3 + 4 + 1 = 8$ $(8 \div 3 = 2 \text{ r } 2)$
4	If the number represented by its last two digits is a multiple of 4, the number is divisible by 4.	728 ✓ $28 \div 4 = 7$ 3,142 ✗ $42 \div 4 = 10 \text{ r } 2$
6	If the number is divisible by both 2 and 3, the number is divisible by 6.	852 ✓ Divisible by 2? The number is even Divisible by 3? $8 + 5 + 2 = 15$ $(15 \div 3 = 5)$ 374 ✗ Divisible by 2? The number is even Divisible by 3? $3 + 7 + 4 = 14$ $(14 \div 3 = 4 \text{ r } 2)$
8	If the number represented by its last three digits is a multiple of 8, the number is divisible by 8.	2,504 ✓ $504 \div 8 = 63$ 2,564 ✗ $564 \div 8 = 70 \text{ r } 4$
9	If the sum of all its digits is a multiple of 9, the number is divisible by 9.	576 ✓ $5 + 7 + 6 = 18$ $(18 \div 9 = 2)$ 1,564 ✗ $1 + 5 + 6 + 4 = 16$ $(16 \div 9 = 1 \text{ r } 7)$
12	If the number is divisible by both 3 and 4, the number is divisible by 12.	648 ✓ Divisible by 3? $6 + 4 + 8 = 18$ $(18 \div 3 = 6)$ Divisible by 4? $48 \div 4 = 12$ 1,746 ✗ Divisible by 3? $1 + 7 + 4 + 6 = 18$ $(18 \div 3 = 6)$ Divisible by 4? $46 \div 4 = 11 \text{ r } 2$

Pages 28-37

Mental multiplication and division

Pages 6-7, 24-27

We can use known number facts, the inverse relationship between multiplication and division, properties of arithmetic, and place value knowledge to solve calculations mentally.

$4 \times 3 = \boxed{12}$ ← product

$12 \div 4 = \boxed{3}$ ← quotient

factor factor

dividend divisor

Multiplication and division are related – they are inverse operations. That means they are opposite operations – multiplication reverses division, and division reverses multiplication.

✕ ⟷ ÷

We can use the following properties of arithmetic to help solve multiplication calculations mentally:

- **commutative property** – changing the order of the factors does not change the product. ← $4 \times 3 = 3 \times 4$

- **associative property** – changing the grouping of the factors does not change the product.

$32 \times 5 = 4 \times 8 \times 5$
$= 4 \times 40$
$= 160$

- **distributive property** – a multiplication calculation can be **partitioned** into the sum of two or more smaller calculations.

$8 \times 64 = (8 \times 60) + (8 \times 4)$
$= 480 + 32$
$= 512$

Understanding and applying compensation strategies can also help us solve calculations mentally.

Compensation strategies involve looking for an easier calculation than the one you need to solve. This could be using a known fact to calculate the answer to an unknown fact, or replacing a number in the calculation with an easier number close to it, and then compensating for this later.

One factor is multiplied by 3, so divide the other factor by 3 to keep the product the same.

$54 \times 6 = \boxed{324}$
$\times 3\downarrow \qquad \downarrow \div 3 \qquad =$
$162 \times 2 = \boxed{324}$

- If one factor is multiplied by a number, and the other factor is divided by the same number, the product stays the same.

These compensation strategies require using your knowledge of inverse operations to calculate the answer.

The amount by which a number is multiplied or divided to increase or decrease a quantity is called the scale factor.

- If one factor is multiplied by a number, the product increases by the same amount.

$$48 \times 5 \ = \boxed{240}$$
$$\times 2 \downarrow \quad \times 2 \downarrow \ \Big) \div 2 =$$
$$48 \times 10 = \boxed{480}$$

> One factor is multiplied by 2 so the product increases by the same scale factor (2). Divide by 2 to calculate the answer.

- If one factor is divided by a number, the product decreases by the same amount.

$$67 \times 4 = \boxed{268}$$
$$\div 2 \downarrow \quad \div 2 \downarrow \ \Big) \times 2 =$$
$$67 \times 2 = \boxed{134}$$

> One factor is divided by 2 so the product decreases by the same scale factor (2). Multiply by 2 to calculate the answer.

- If the dividend is multiplied by a number, and the divisor is kept the same, the quotient increases by the same amount.

$$425 \div 5 = \boxed{85}$$
$$\times 2 \downarrow \quad \times 2 \downarrow \ \Big) \div 2 =$$
$$850 \div 5 = \boxed{170}$$

> The dividend is multiplied by 2 so the quotient increases by the same scale factor (2). Divide by 2 to calculate the answer.

- If the dividend is divided by a number, and the divisor is kept the same, the quotient decreases by the same amount.

$$486 \div 3 = \boxed{162}$$
$$\downarrow \div 2 \quad \div 2 \downarrow \ \Big) \times 2 =$$
$$243 \div 3 = \boxed{81}$$

> The dividend is divided by 2 so the quotient decreases by the same scale factor (2). Multiply by 2 to calculate the answer.

- If the divisor is multiplied by a number, and the dividend is kept the same, the quotient decreases by the same amount.

$$460 \div 5 \ = \boxed{92}$$
$$\times 2 \downarrow \quad \div 2 \downarrow \ \Big) \times 2 =$$
$$460 \div 10 = \boxed{46}$$

> The divisor is multiplied by 2 so the quotient decreases by the same scale factor (2). Multiply by 2 to calculate the answer.

- If the divisor is divided by a number, and the dividend is kept the same, the quotient increases by the same amount.

$$312 \div 12 = \boxed{26}$$
$$\div 4 \downarrow \quad \times 4 \downarrow \ \Big) \div 4 =$$
$$312 \div 3 \ = \boxed{104}$$

> The divisor is divided by 4 so the quotient increases by the same scale factor (4). Divide by 4 to calculate the answer.

Pages 30-37, 58-59, 68-71, 92-93

Multiply up to a 4-digit number by a 1-digit number

Pages 6-9, 12-13, 24-29

We can use our understanding of place value and multiplication tables facts to multiply a 2-, 3- or 4-digit number by a 1-digit number, such as 2,654 × 3.

2,654 × 3 = 7,962

⚠ **ALWAYS:**
Estimate **C**alculate **C**heck

Step 1: Set out the calculation.

×	2,000	600	50	4
3				

As we are multiplying 2,654 by 3, **partition** 3 lots of 2,654 into **thousands**, **hundreds**, tens and ones.

Step 2: Multiply the ones.

×	2,000	600	50	4
3				

4 ones **multiplied by** 3 (4 × 3). As there are more than 10 ones, we need to **regroup** 10 ones into 1 ten.

Step 3: Multiply the tens.

×	2,000	600	50	4
3				

5 tens multiplied by 3 (50 × 3). As there are more than 10 tens, we need to regroup 10 tens into 1 **hundred**.

Step 4: Multiply the hundreds.

×	2,000	600	50	4
3				

6 **hundreds** multiplied by 3 (600 × 3). As there are more than 10 **hundreds**, we need to regroup 10 **hundreds** into 1 **thousand**.

Step 5: Multiply the thousands.

×	2,000	600	50	4
3				

2 thousands multiplied by 3 (2,000 × 3).

Step 6: Combine the thousands, hundreds, tens and ones.

×	2,000	600	50	4
3				

7 thousands + 9 hundreds + 6 tens + 2 ones = 7,962
7,000 + 900 + 60 + 2 = 7,962

We can record this calculation in different ways.

Grid method

×	2,000	600	50	4
3	6,000	1,800	150	12	= 7,962

Partitioning method

$2{,}654 \times 3 = (2{,}000 \times 3) + (600 \times 3) + (50 \times 3) + (4 \times 3)$

$\qquad = 6{,}000 + 1{,}800 + 150 + 12$

$\qquad = 7{,}962$

What's the same about each of these methods?

What's different?

Which method do you prefer? Why?

Expanded written method

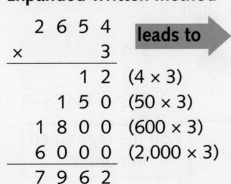

```
    2 6 5 4
×         3
        1 2   (4 × 3)
      1 5 0   (50 × 3)
    1 8 0 0   (600 × 3)
    6 0 0 0   (2,000 × 3)
    7 9 6 2
```

leads to

Formal written method of short multiplication

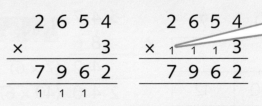

```
    2 6 5 4          2 6 5 4
×         3      × ₁ ₁ ₁ 3
    7 9 6 2          7 9 6 2
  ₁ ₁ ₁
```

You can also write the regrouped values like this.

Pages 32–33, 70–71, 82–83

Multiply up to a 4-digit number by a 2-digit number

Pages 6-9, 12-13, 24-31

To multiply a 2-, 3- or 4-digit number by a 2-digit number, we can partition both numbers, multiply each of the digits in one factor by each of the digits in the other factor, and then add the partial products.

547 × 86 = 47,042

factor   product

547 × 86 = 47,042

factor

⚠ ALWAYS:
Estimate
Calculate
Check

Step 1: Set out the calculation.

and Step 2: Multiply the ones **digit by the** ones **digit.**

Expanded written method	Formal written method of long multiplication

Grid method

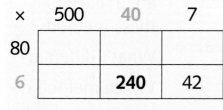

```
    5 4 7
  ×   8 6      leads to
    4 2  (7 × 6)
```

```
    5 4 7
  ×   8 6
    ₄2  (547 × 6)
```

Regroup the 4 tens.

Step 3: Multiply the tens **digit by the** ones **digit.**

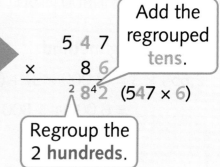

```
    5 4 7
  ×   8 6      leads to
    4 2  (7 × 6)
  2 4 0  (40 × 6)
```

Add the regrouped tens.

```
    5 4 7
  ×   8 6
  ₂8₄2  (547 × 6)
```

Regroup the 2 hundreds.

Step 4: Multiply the hundreds **digit by the** ones **digit.**

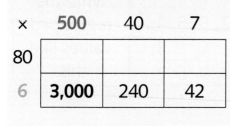

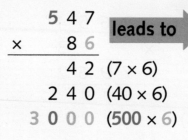

```
    5 4 7
  ×   8 6      leads to
    4 2  (7 × 6)
  2 4 0  (40 × 6)
3 0 0 0  (500 × 6)
```

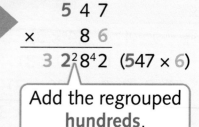

Add the regrouped hundreds.

Step 5: Multiply the ones digit by the tens digit.

×	500	40	7
80			**560**
6	3,000	240	42

$$
\begin{array}{r}
5\ 4\ 7 \\
\times \quad 8\ 6 \\
\hline
4\ 2 \quad (7 \times 6) \\
2\ 4\ 0 \quad (40 \times 6) \\
3\ 0\ 0\ 0 \quad (500 \times 6) \\
5\ 6\ 0 \quad (7 \times 80) \\
\end{array}
$$

leads to

$$
\begin{array}{r}
5\ 4\ 7 \\
\times \quad 8\ 6 \\
\hline
3\ 2^2 8^4 2 \quad (547 \times 6) \\
{}^5 6\ 0 \quad (547 \times 80) \\
\end{array}
$$

Write a **zero** to show it's 10 times the size.

Regroup the 5 **hundreds**.

Step 6: Multiply the tens digit by the tens digit.

×	500	40	7
80		**3,200**	560
6	3,000	240	42

$$
\begin{array}{r}
5\ 4\ 7 \\
\times \quad 8\ 6 \\
\hline
4\ 2 \quad (7 \times 6) \\
2\ 4\ 0 \quad (40 \times 6) \\
3\ 0\ 0\ 0 \quad (500 \times 6) \\
5\ 6\ 0 \quad (7 \times 80) \\
3\ 2\ 0\ 0 \quad (40 \times 80) \\
\end{array}
$$

leads to

$$
\begin{array}{r}
5\ 4\ 7 \\
\times \quad 8\ 6 \\
\hline
3\ 2^2 8^4 2 \quad (547 \times 6) \\
{}^3 7^5 6\ 0 \quad (547 \times 80) \\
\end{array}
$$

Add the regrouped **hundreds**.

Regroup the 3 thousands.

Step 7: Multiply the hundreds digit by the tens digit.

×	500	40	7
80	**40,000**	3,200	560
6	3,000	240	42

$$
\begin{array}{r}
5\ 4\ 7 \\
\times \quad 8\ 6 \\
\hline
4\ 2 \quad (7 \times 6) \\
2\ 4\ 0 \quad (40 \times 6) \\
3\ 0\ 0\ 0 \quad (500 \times 6) \\
5\ 6\ 0 \quad (7 \times 80) \\
3\ 2\ 0\ 0 \quad (40 \times 80) \\
4\ 0\ 0\ 0\ 0 \quad (500 \times 80) \\
\end{array}
$$

leads to

$$
\begin{array}{r}
5\ 4\ 7 \\
\times \quad 8\ 6 \\
\hline
3\ 2^2 8^4 2 \quad (547 \times 6) \\
4\ 3^3 7^5 6\ 0 \quad (547 \times 80) \\
\end{array}
$$

Add the regrouped thousands.

Step 8: Add the partial products.

×	500	40	7
80	40,000	3,200	560
6	3,000	240	42

43,760 + 3,282 = 47,042

$$
\begin{array}{r}
5\ 4\ 7 \\
\times \quad 8\ 6 \\
\hline
4\ 2 \quad (7 \times 6) \\
2\ 4\ 0 \quad (40 \times 6) \\
3\ 0\ 0\ 0 \quad (500 \times 6) \\
5\ 6\ 0 \quad (7 \times 80) \\
3\ 2\ 0\ 0 \quad (40 \times 80) \\
4\ 0\ 0\ 0\ 0 \quad (500 \times 80) \\
\hline
\mathbf{4\ 7\ 0\ 4\ 2} \\
1 \quad 1
\end{array}
$$

leads to

$$
\begin{array}{r}
5\ 4\ 7 \\
\times \quad 8\ 6 \\
\hline
3\ 2^2 8^4 2 \quad (547 \times 6) \\
4\ 3^3 7^5 6\ 0 \quad (547 \times 80) \\
\hline
\mathbf{4\ 7\ 0\ 4\ 2} \\
1\ \ 1
\end{array}
$$

Pages 70-71, 82-83

Divide a 3- or 4-digit number by a 1-digit number

Pages 6–9, 12–13, 24–29

We can use our understanding of place value and multiplication and division facts to divide a 3- or 4-digit number by a 1-digit number.

$3{,}741 \div 6 = \boxed{623 \text{ r } 3} \text{ or } \boxed{623\frac{1}{2}} \text{ or } \boxed{623 \cdot 5}$

⚠ **ALWAYS:**
Estimate   **C**alculate   **C**heck

Step 1: Set out the calculation.

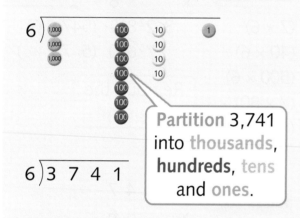

Partition 3,741 into thousands, hundreds, tens and ones.

$6\overline{)3\ 7\ 4\ 1}$

Step 2: Share the thousands.

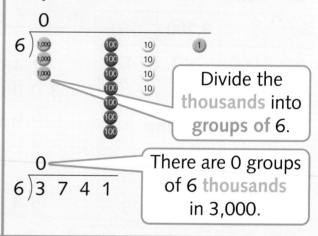

Divide the thousands into groups of 6.

There are 0 groups of 6 thousands in 3,000.

$\dfrac{0}{6\overline{)3\ 7\ 4\ 1}}$

Step 3: Exchange the thousands.

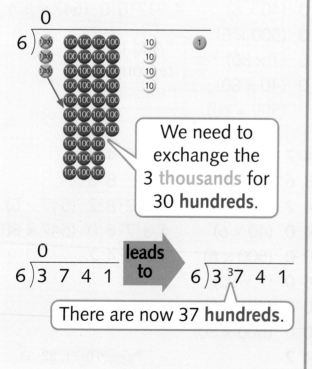

We need to exchange the 3 thousands for 30 hundreds.

$\dfrac{0}{6\overline{)3\ 7\ 4\ 1}}$ **leads to** $6\overline{)3\ ^37\ 4\ 1}$

There are now 37 hundreds.

Step 4: Share the hundreds.

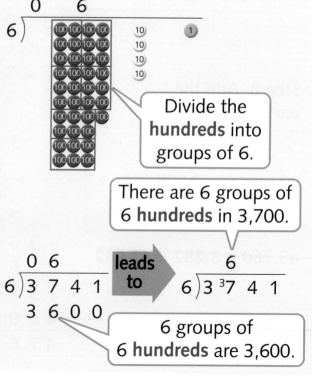

Divide the hundreds into groups of 6.

There are 6 groups of 6 hundreds in 3,700.

$\begin{array}{r} 0\ 6 \\ 6\overline{)3\ 7\ 4\ 1} \\ 3\ 6\ 0\ 0 \end{array}$ **leads to** $\dfrac{6}{6\overline{)3\ ^37\ 4\ 1}}$

6 groups of 6 hundreds are 3,600.

34

Step 5: Exchange the hundreds.

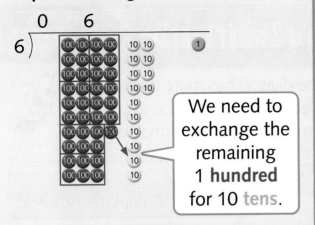

We need to exchange the remaining 1 **hundred** for 10 tens.

$$
\begin{array}{r}
0\ 6 \\
6\overline{)3\ 7\ 4\ 1} \\
-\ 3\ 6\ 0\ 0 \\
\hline
1\ 4\ 1
\end{array}
$$

leads to

$$
6\overline{)3\ {}^3 7\ {}^1 4\ 1}
$$

There are now 14 tens.

Step 6: Share the tens.

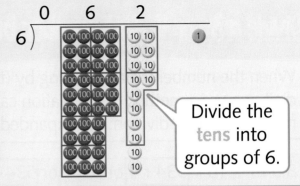

Divide the tens into groups of 6.

There are 2 groups of 6 tens in 140.

$$
\begin{array}{r}
0\ 6\ 2 \\
6\overline{)3\ 7\ 4\ 1} \\
-\ 3\ 6\ 0\ 0 \\
\hline
1\ 4\ 1 \\
1\ 2\ 0
\end{array}
$$

leads to

$$
6\overline{)3\ {}^3 7\ {}^1 4\ 1}
$$

2 groups of 6 tens are 120.

Step 7: Exchange the tens.

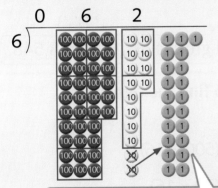

We need to exchange the remaining 2 tens for 20 ones.

$$
\begin{array}{r}
0\ 6\ 2 \\
6\overline{)3\ 7\ 4\ 1} \\
-\ 3\ 6\ 0\ 0 \\
\hline
1\ 4\ 1 \\
-\ \ 1\ 2\ 0 \\
\hline
2\ 1
\end{array}
$$

leads to

$$
6\overline{)3\ {}^3 7\ {}^1 4\ {}^2 1}
$$

There are now 21 ones.

Step 8: Share the ones.

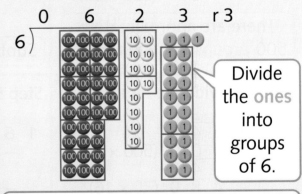

Divide the ones into groups of 6.

There are 3 groups of 6 ones in 21.

$$
\begin{array}{r}
0\ 6\ 2\ 3\ r\,3 \\
6\overline{)3\ 7\ 4\ 1} \\
-\ 3\ 6\ 0\ 0 \\
\hline
1\ 4\ 1 \\
-\quad 1\ 2\ 0 \\
\hline
2\ 1 \\
-\quad\ \ 1\ 8 \\
\hline
3
\end{array}
$$

leads to

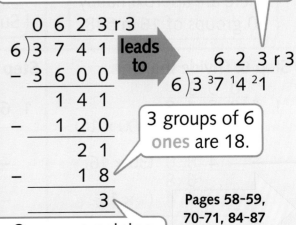

3 groups of 6 ones are 18.

There are 3 ones remaining.

Pages 58-59, 70-71, 84-87

Divide a 3- or 4-digit number by a 2-digit number

Pages 6-9, 12-13, 24-29, 34-35

When the number we are dividing by (the divisor) has more than one digit, we use a method of calculation called long division. There are two methods of long division: the expanded method and the formal method.

$8{,}548 \div 16 = \boxed{534 \text{ r } 4}$ or $\boxed{534\frac{1}{4}}$ or $\boxed{534 \cdot 25}$

⚠ ALWAYS:
Estimate **C**alculate **C**heck

Expanded method

Step 1: Set out the calculation.

$$16\,\overline{)8\ 5\ 4\ 8}$$

$1 \times 16 = 16$
$2 \times 16 = 32$
$3 \times 16 = 48$
$4 \times 16 = 64$
$5 \times 16 = 80$

Writing out multiples of the divisor helps us carry out the calculation.

Use your knowledge of multiplying by 10 and 100, e.g. $30 \times 16 = 480$.

Step 2: Divide the thousands.

$$\begin{array}{r} 0\ 5 \\ 16\,\overline{)8\ 5\ 4\ 8} \\ 8\ 0\ 0\ 0 \quad (500 \times 16) \end{array}$$

There are approximately 500 groups of 16 in 8,548.

Step 3: Subtract to find the remainder.

$$\begin{array}{r} 0\ 5 \\ 16\,\overline{)8\ 5\ 4\ 8} \\ -\ 8\ 0\ 0\ 0 \quad (500 \times 16) \\ \hline 5\ 4\ 8 \end{array}$$

Subtract the 500 groups of 16 from 8,548.

Step 4: Divide the hundreds.

$$\begin{array}{r} 0\ 5\ 3 \\ 16\,\overline{)8\ 5\ 4\ 8} \\ -\ 8\ 0\ 0\ 0 \quad (500 \times 16) \\ \hline 5\ 4\ 8 \\ 4\ 8\ 0 \quad (30 \times 16) \end{array}$$

There are approximately 30 groups of 16 in 548.

Step 5: Subtract to find the remainder.

$$\begin{array}{r} 0\ 5\ 3 \\ 16\,\overline{)8\ 5\ 4\ 8} \\ -\ 8\ 0\ 0\ 0 \quad (500 \times 16) \\ {}^4\!5\,{}^1\!4\ 8 \\ -\ \ 4\ 8\ 0 \quad (30 \times 16) \\ \hline 6\ 8 \end{array}$$

Subtract the 30 groups of 16 from 548.

Step 6: Divide the tens.

$$\begin{array}{r} 0\ 5\ 3\ 4 \\ 16\,\overline{)8\ 5\ 4\ 8} \\ -\ 8\ 0\ 0\ 0 \quad (500 \times 16) \\ {}^4\!5\,{}^1\!4\ 8 \\ -\ \ 4\ 8\ 0 \quad (30 \times 16) \\ \hline 6\ 8 \\ 6\ 4 \quad (4 \times 16) \end{array}$$

There are approximately 4 groups of 16 in 68.

Step 7: Subtract to find the remainder.

$$\begin{array}{r} 0\ 5\ 3\ 4 \text{ r } 4 \\ 16\,\overline{)8\ 5\ 4\ 8} \\ -\ 8\ 0\ 0\ 0 \quad (500 \times 16) \\ {}^4\!5\,{}^1\!4\ 8 \\ -\ \ 4\ 8\ 0 \quad (30 \times 16) \\ \hline 6\ 8 \\ -\ \ 6\ 4 \quad (4 \times 16) \\ \hline 4 \end{array}$$

Subtract the 4 groups of 16 from 68. That leaves a remainder of 4.

Formal method

Step 1: Set out the calculation.

$$16 \overline{)8\ 5\ 4\ 8}$$

Step 2: Divide the thousands.

$$16 \overline{)\overset{0}{8}\ 5\ 4\ 8}$$

8 thousands ÷ 16 = 0 thousands r 8 thousands

Step 3: Exchange thousands for hundreds, combine with the existing hundreds and divide.

$$16 \overline{)\overset{0\ 5}{8\ 5\ 4\ 8}} \\ \ \ \ 8\ 0$$

85 hundreds ÷ 16 = 5 hundreds and a remainder

5 hundreds × 16 = 80 hundreds

Step 4: Subtract to find the remainder.

$$16 \overline{)\overset{0\ 5}{8\ 5\ 4\ 8}} \\ -\ \ 8\ 0 \\ \ \ \ \ \ \ 5$$

Step 5: Exchange hundreds for tens and combine with the existing tens.

$$16 \overline{)\overset{0\ 5}{8\ 5\ 4\ 8}} \\ -\ 8\ 0\ \downarrow \\ \ \ \ \ 5\ 4$$

5 hundreds = 50 tens
50 tens + 4 tens = 54 tens

Step 6: Divide the tens.

$$16 \overline{)\overset{0\ 5\ 3}{8\ 5\ 4\ 8}} \\ -\ 8\ 0\ \downarrow \\ \ \ \ \ 5\ 4 \\ \ \ \ \ 4\ 8$$

54 tens ÷ 16 = 3 tens and a remainder

Step 7: Subtract to find the remainder.

$$16 \overline{)\overset{0\ 5\ 3}{8\ 5\ 4\ 8}} \\ -\ 8\ 0\ \downarrow \\ \ \ \ \ {}^4\!\!\not{5}\,{}^1 4 \\ -\ \ \ \ 4\ 8 \\ \ \ \ \ \ \ \ 6$$

Step 8: Exchange tens for ones and combine with the existing ones.

$$16 \overline{)\overset{0\ 5\ 3}{8\ 5\ 4\ 8}} \\ -\ 8\ 0\ \downarrow \\ \ \ \ \ {}^4\!\!\not{5}\,{}^1 4\ \downarrow \\ -\ \ \ \ 4\ 8\ \downarrow \\ \ \ \ \ \ \ \ 6\ 8$$

6 tens = 60 ones
60 ones + 8 ones = 68 ones

Step 9: Divide the ones.

$$16 \overline{)\overset{0\ 5\ 3\ 4}{8\ 5\ 4\ 8}} \\ -\ 8\ 0\ \downarrow \\ \ \ \ \ {}^4\!\!\not{5}\,{}^1 4 \\ -\ \ \ \ 4\ 8\ \downarrow \\ \ \ \ \ \ \ \ 6\ 8 \\ \ \ \ \ \ \ \ 6\ 4$$

68 ones ÷ 16 = 4 ones and a remainder

Step 10: Subtract to find the remainder.

$$16 \overline{)\overset{0\ 5\ 3\ 4\ r\,4}{8\ 5\ 4\ 8}} \\ -\ 8\ 0\ \downarrow \\ \ \ \ \ {}^4\!\!\not{5}\,{}^1 4 \\ -\ \ \ \ 4\ 8 \\ \ \ \ \ \ \ \ 6\ 8 \\ -\ \ \ \ \ 6\ 4 \\ \ \ \ \ \ \ \ \ \ 4$$

Pages 58-59, 70-71, 84-87

Order of operations and using brackets

Some calculations involve more than just two numbers with one operation. Sometimes we need to carry out calculations where there are several different operations to do. It's important that we know which order to do them in so that we get the correct answer.

Numerical operations include **addition** (+), **subtraction** (−), **multiplication** (×) and **division** (÷).

But what do you do when a **calculation** involves more than one operation?

Look at this calculation: $4 \times (8 + 13) =$
Which part of the calculation do you calculate first?

Without knowing the **order of operations**, different people may interpret a calculation in different ways and come up with different answers.

So, in order to avoid this, a collection of rules was established.

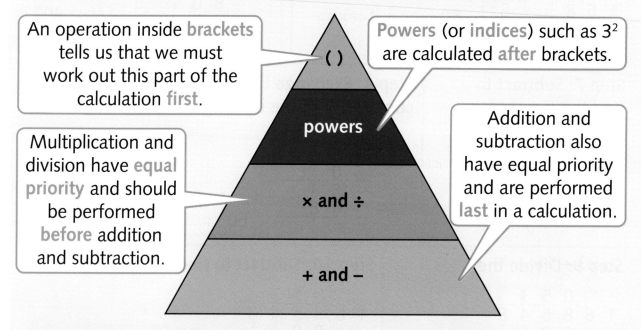

An operation inside **brackets** tells us that we must work out this part of the calculation **first**.

Powers (or **indices**) such as 3^2 are calculated **after** brackets.

Multiplication and division have **equal priority** and should be performed **before** addition and subtraction.

Addition and subtraction also have equal priority and are performed **last** in a calculation.

( )

powers

× and ÷

+ and −

A way to remember the order of operations is to use the word BODMAS (or BIDMAS).

It stands for **B**rackets, followed by **O**rders (or **I**ndices), then **D**ivision and **M**ultiplication, and finally **A**ddition and **S**ubtraction.

We should always work out calculations in this order, even if they are ordered differently when the calculation is written down.

Let's look back at the calculation: $4 \times (8 + 13) =$

First, perform the operation in the brackets: $4 \times (8 + 13)$

Then, multiply the sum: $4 \times 21 = 84$

Look at each pair of calculations.

$5 + 6 \times 3$	$10 + 8 \div 2$	$18 - 9 \div 3$
$= 5 + 18$	$= 10 + 4$	$= 18 - 3$
$= 23$	$= 14$	$= 15$
$(5 + 6) \times 3$	$(10 + 8) \div 2$	$(18 - 9) \div 3$
$= 11 \times 3$	$= 18 \div 2$	$= 9 \div 3$
$= 33$	$= 9$	$= 3$

What's the same about each pair of calculations? What's different?

Now look at these calculations that include powers.

$5^2 - 2 \times 8$	$6^2 \div (14 - 5)$	$(8 + 4)^2$
$= 25 - 16$	$= 36 \div 9$	$= 12^2$
$= 9$	$= 4$	$= 144$

These calculations include more numbers and operations, but we still apply the same rules for the order of operations.

$5 \times 4 + 7 \times 2$	$5 \times 4 - 7 \times 2$	$5 \times (4 + 7) \times 2$
$= 20 + 14$	$= 20 - 14$	$= 5 \times 11 \times 2$
$= 34$	$= 6$	$= 110$

There is another rule, or convention about the order of operations.

If there is no operation sign written, this means multiply.

So, $3(5 + 4) = 3 \times (5 + 4)$

$= 3 \times 9$

$= 27$

Simplify fractions

Pages 24-25

We can simplify fractions by reducing the size of the numerator and denominator to make an equivalent fraction that's easier to work with.

Let's look at the fraction: $\frac{16}{24}$.

When we divide both the numerator and the denominator by 2, we make the equivalent fraction $\frac{8}{12}$.

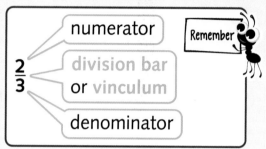

numerator

Remember

$\frac{2}{3}$ — division bar or vinculum

denominator

Divide the numerator by 2.

$$\frac{16}{24} \overset{\div 2}{=} \frac{8}{12}$$

Divide the denominator by 2. $\div 2$

If we keep dividing the numerator and denominator by 2, we end up with $\frac{2}{3}$.

We can't simplify $\frac{2}{3}$ any further.

$$\frac{16}{24} \overset{\div 2}{\underset{\div 2}{=}} \frac{8}{12} \overset{\div 2}{\underset{\div 2}{=}} \frac{4}{6} \overset{\div 2}{\underset{\div 2}{=}} \frac{2}{3}$$

So, $\frac{16}{24}$ in its simplest form is $\frac{2}{3}$.

We can use a fraction wall to show this.

1

$\frac{2}{3}$ — $\frac{1}{3}$

$\frac{4}{6}$ — $\frac{1}{6}$

$\frac{8}{12}$ — $\frac{1}{12}$

$\frac{16}{24}$ — $\frac{1}{24}$

Look back at the model on page 40. We can see that a simpler method of simplifying $\frac{16}{24}$ would be to divide both the numerator and denominator by 8.

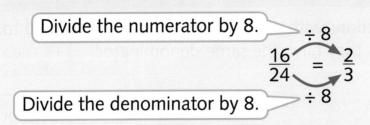

Divide the numerator by 8.

$$\frac{16}{24} = \frac{2}{3}$$

Divide the denominator by 8.

Instead of having to divide the numerator and denominator several times to simplify a fraction, we can do this by dividing both the numerator and denominator by their highest common factor (HCF).

So, another method of simplifying $\frac{16}{24}$ is to divide both the numerator and the denominator by their highest common factor.

We list all the factors of the numerator, 16.

Factors of 16: 1, 2, 4, 8 and 16

We also list all the factors of the denominator, 24.

Factors of 24: 1, 2, 3, 4, 6, 8 , 12 and 24

The common factors of 16 and 24 are 1, 2, 4 and 8.

The highest common factor of 16 and 24 is 8.

Now, if we divide the numerator and denominator by 8, we get $\frac{2}{3}$.

$$\frac{16}{24} = \frac{2}{3}$$

Therefore, $\frac{2}{3}$ is the simplest fraction we can make from $\frac{16}{24}$.

 Use your preferred method to write each of these fractions in its simplest form.

| $\frac{6}{12}$ | $\frac{5}{15}$ | $\frac{2}{8}$ | $\frac{4}{12}$ | $\frac{12}{16}$ | $\frac{6}{15}$ |

Pages 42–57, 90–91

Express fractions with the same denominator

Pages 24-25, 40-41

To compare fractions with different denominators we need to express them so they have the same denominator.

Look at these two fractions: $\frac{1}{4}$ $\frac{5}{12}$

They have different denominators.

We can express these fractions with a common denominator.

12 is a multiple of 4.

That means we can use 12 as the common denominator.

We need to express both fractions in twelfths.

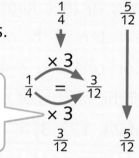

numerator

division bar or vinculum

denominator

$\frac{5}{12}$

Remember

$\frac{1}{4}$ $\frac{5}{12}$

$\times 3$

$\frac{1}{4} = \frac{3}{12}$

$\times 3$

$\frac{3}{12}$ $\frac{5}{12}$

We multiply the numerator and denominator by 3 to change $\frac{1}{4}$ to the equivalent fraction $\frac{3}{12}$.

Now look at these two fractions: $\frac{1}{3}$ $\frac{2}{7}$

What do you notice about the denominators of the two fractions?
One denominator is not a multiple of the other.
We need to identify the lowest common multiple (LCM) of the two denominators.

Multiples of 3: 3, 6, 9, 12, 15, 18, 21 , ...   Multiples of 7: 7, 14, 21 , ...

The lowest common multiple of 3 and 7 is 21.
So 21 is the lowest common denominator (LCD) of $\frac{1}{3}$ and $\frac{2}{7}$.
We need to express both fractions in twenty-firsts.

We multiply the numerator and denominator by 7 to change $\frac{1}{3}$ to the equivalent fraction $\frac{7}{21}$.

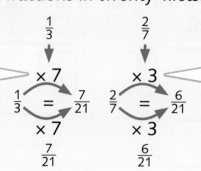

$\frac{1}{3}$ $\frac{2}{7}$

$\times 7$ $\times 3$

$\frac{1}{3} = \frac{7}{21}$ $\frac{2}{7} = \frac{6}{21}$

$\times 7$ $\times 3$

$\frac{7}{21}$ $\frac{6}{21}$

We multiply the numerator and denominator by 3 to change $\frac{2}{7}$ to the equivalent fraction $\frac{6}{21}$.

Let's look again at the fractions $\frac{1}{3}$ and $\frac{2}{7}$ and their equivalent fractions with common denominators.

$$\frac{1}{3} = \frac{7}{21} \qquad \frac{2}{7} = \frac{6}{21}$$

What do you notice about how the denominator 21 relates to the denominators 3 and 7?

When one denominator is not a multiple of the other, we can multiply the two denominators to find a common denominator.

Look at these two fractions: $\frac{2}{3}$ $\frac{3}{5}$

One denominator is not a multiple of the other.

We can express both fractions with a common denominator by multiplying the two denominators. $\boxed{3 \times 5 = 15}$

15 is a multiple of both 3 and 5.

We can use 15 as the common denominator.

We need to express both fractions in fifteenths.

Look at these two fractions: $\frac{1}{6}$ $\frac{4}{9}$

One denominator is not a multiple of the other.

How can both fractions be expressed with a common denominator?

We can express both fractions with a common denominator by multiplying the two denominators: $\boxed{6 \times 9 = 54}$

Does this method result in the lowest common denominator?

When expressing fractions with a common denominator, we should always try to identify the lowest common denominator.

 Write

Express each set of fractions with a common denominator.

$\frac{2}{3}$ $\frac{1}{2}$ $\frac{3}{4}$	$\frac{2}{3}$ $\frac{3}{5}$ $\frac{4}{15}$	$\frac{1}{4}$ $\frac{3}{5}$ $\frac{1}{2}$

Pages 44–51, 86–87, 90–91

43

Compare and order fractions

Pages 40-43

To compare and order fractions, we look at the numerators and denominators of the fractions and apply knowledge of equivalent fractions. Like with whole numbers, we can use the inequality symbols < and > to compare and order fractions.

We can order fractions:

in ascending order – from smallest to largest/greatest

or in descending order – from largest/greatest to smallest.

A proper fraction is a fraction with a value less than 1, where the numerator is less than the denominator.

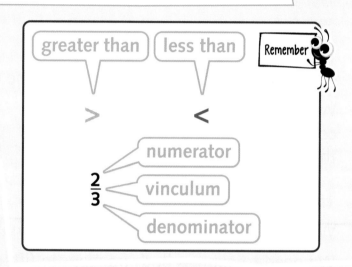

greater than | less than | Remember

$>$ $<$

$\frac{2}{3}$ — numerator / vinculum / denominator

When comparing and ordering proper fractions with the same denominator, the greater the numerator, the greater the fraction.

5 sixths is greater than 2 sixths.
$\frac{5}{6} > \frac{2}{6}$

2 sixths is 2 lots of 1 sixth.

| $\frac{1}{6}$ | $\frac{1}{6}$ | $\frac{1}{6}$ | $\frac{1}{6}$ | $\frac{1}{6}$ | $\frac{1}{6}$ |

5 sixths is 5 lots of 1 sixth.

| $\frac{1}{6}$ | $\frac{1}{6}$ | $\frac{1}{6}$ | $\frac{1}{6}$ | $\frac{1}{6}$ | $\frac{1}{6}$ |

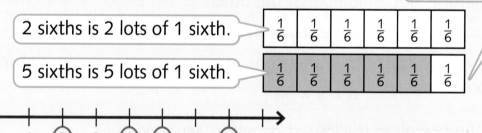

0 $\frac{1}{8}$ $\frac{2}{8}$ $\frac{3}{8}$ $\frac{4}{8}$ $\frac{5}{8}$ $\frac{6}{8}$ $\frac{7}{8}$ 1

$\frac{2}{8} < \frac{4}{8} < \frac{5}{8} < \frac{7}{8}$

When comparing and ordering fractions, if the numerators are all 1 (unit fractions), then the greater the denominator, the smaller the fraction.

The denominator represents the number of equal parts the whole has been divided into. The greater this number, the more equal parts and therefore the smaller the size of each part.

1 seventh is smaller than 1 fifth.
$\frac{1}{7} < \frac{1}{5}$

| $\frac{1}{7}$ | $\frac{1}{7}$ | $\frac{1}{7}$ | $\frac{1}{7}$ | $\frac{1}{7}$ | $\frac{1}{7}$ | $\frac{1}{7}$ |

| $\frac{1}{5}$ | $\frac{1}{5}$ | $\frac{1}{5}$ | $\frac{1}{5}$ | $\frac{1}{5}$ |

Look at these models and fractions. They all have a numerator of 1.

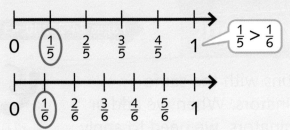

$\frac{1}{5} > \frac{1}{6}$

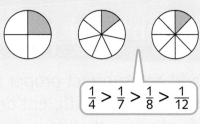

$\frac{1}{4} > \frac{1}{7} > \frac{1}{8} > \frac{1}{12}$

When comparing and ordering fractions, if the numerators are all the same, then the greater the denominator, the smaller the fraction.

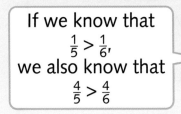

If we know that
$\frac{1}{5} > \frac{1}{6}$,
we also know that
$\frac{4}{5} > \frac{4}{6}$

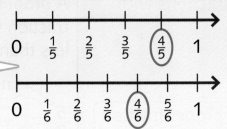

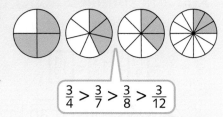

$\frac{3}{4} > \frac{3}{7} > \frac{3}{8} > \frac{3}{12}$

When comparing and ordering fractions, if the denominators are different, we need to convert them to equivalent fractions with a common denominator.

Which is greater, $\frac{2}{6}$ or $\frac{3}{5}$?

We know that $\frac{2}{6} = \frac{1}{3}$.

Find equivalent fractions: $\frac{1}{3} \overset{\times 5}{\underset{\times 5}{=}} \frac{5}{15}$ $\frac{3}{5} \overset{\times 3}{\underset{\times 3}{=}} \frac{9}{15}$

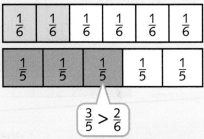

$\frac{3}{5} > \frac{2}{6}$

When we look at the fractions $\frac{2}{6}$ and $\frac{3}{5}$ we can see that 3 is a greater part of 5 than 2 is of 6, which means that $\frac{3}{5}$ is greater than $\frac{2}{6}$.

When we compare and order mixed numbers, we compare the whole number part first, then the fractional part.

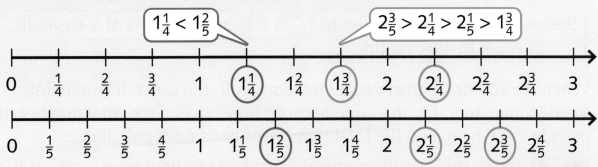

$1\frac{1}{4} < 1\frac{2}{5}$

$2\frac{3}{5} > 2\frac{1}{4} > 2\frac{1}{5} > 1\frac{3}{4}$

Pages 62-63, 90-91

Fractions

Add and subtract proper fractions

Pages 24-25, 40-43

We can add and subtract proper fractions with the same denominators or with different denominators. When we add or subtract fractions with different denominators, we need to apply our knowledge of equivalent fractions.

Add and subtract proper fractions with the same denominator

$\frac{5}{9} + \frac{7}{9} = \boxed{\frac{12}{9}} = \boxed{1\frac{3}{9}} = \boxed{1\frac{1}{3}}$

Always convert an improper fraction to a mixed number and reduce a fraction to its simplest form.

A proper fraction is a fraction with a numerator less than its denominator.

numerator

Remember

$\frac{5}{7}$ vinculum

denominator

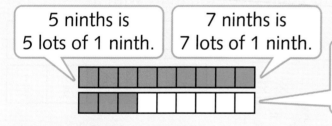

5 ninths is 5 lots of 1 ninth.

7 ninths is 7 lots of 1 ninth.

5 ninths add 7 ninths is equal to 12 ninths, which is also equal to 1 whole and 3 ninths.

$\frac{9}{11} - \frac{5}{11} = \boxed{\frac{4}{11}}$

9 elevenths is 9 lots of 1 eleventh.

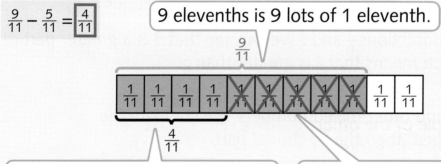

9 elevenths subtract 5 elevenths is equal to 4 elevenths.

5 elevenths is 5 lots of 1 eleventh.

When we add or subtract proper fractions with the same denominator, the denominators stay the same because they tell you the total number of parts in the whole, and the total number of parts does not change.

We just add or subtract the numerators to find out how many parts of the whole there are.

Add and subtract proper fractions with different denominators

Unlike fractions are fractions with different denominators. To add or subtract them, we need to convert one or both of the fractions to an **equivalent fraction** so that both fractions have a **common denominator**.

$$\frac{1}{3} + \frac{2}{5} = \boxed{\frac{11}{15}}$$

One denominator is not a **multiple** of the other.

We need to identify a common denominator of the two fractions.

Multiples of 3: 3, 6, 9, 12, $\boxed{15}$, ...   Multiples of 5: 5, 10, $\boxed{15}$, ...

The **lowest common multiple** (**LCM**) of 3 and 5 is 15.

So, 15 is the **lowest common denominator** (**LCD**) of $\frac{1}{3}$ and $\frac{2}{5}$.

We need to express both fractions in fifteenths.

$$\frac{1}{3} \quad + \quad \frac{2}{5} \quad = \qquad \frac{1}{3} + \frac{2}{5} = \frac{5}{15} + \frac{6}{15}$$

$$= \frac{11}{15}$$

$$\overset{\times 5}{\underset{\times 5}{\frac{1}{3} = \frac{5}{15}}} \qquad \overset{\times 3}{\underset{\times 3}{\frac{2}{5} = \frac{6}{15}}}$$

$$\frac{9}{10} - \frac{2}{3} = \boxed{\frac{7}{30}}$$

We apply the same process when subtracting proper fractions with different denominators.

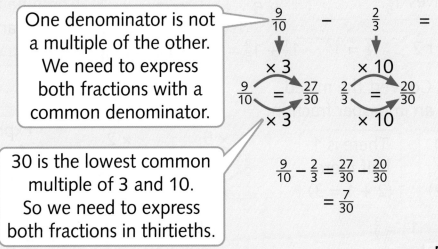

One denominator is not a multiple of the other. We need to express both fractions with a common denominator.

$$\frac{9}{10} \quad - \quad \frac{2}{3} \quad =$$

$$\overset{\times 3}{\underset{\times 3}{\frac{9}{10} = \frac{27}{30}}} \qquad \overset{\times 10}{\underset{\times 10}{\frac{2}{3} = \frac{20}{30}}}$$

30 is the lowest common multiple of 3 and 10. So we need to express both fractions in thirtieths.

$$\frac{9}{10} - \frac{2}{3} = \frac{27}{30} - \frac{20}{30}$$

$$= \frac{7}{30}$$

Pages 48–53

Add mixed numbers

Pages 24-25, 40-43, 46-47

To add two fractions where one or both are mixed numbers or improper fractions, we apply our knowledge of converting between mixed numbers and improper fractions, and of finding equivalent fractions with common denominators.

Add two improper fractions

$\frac{3}{2} + \frac{6}{5} = \boxed{2\frac{7}{10}}$

> One **denominator** is not a **multiple** of the other. So, we need to **express** both **fractions** in tenths.

How else could you solve this fraction addition?

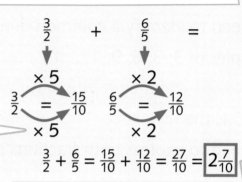

$\frac{3}{2} + \frac{6}{5} = \frac{15}{10} + \frac{12}{10} = \frac{27}{10} = \boxed{2\frac{7}{10}}$

> **Convert** the **improper fraction** $\frac{27}{10}$ to the **mixed number** $2\frac{7}{10}$.

Add an improper fraction to a mixed number

$1\frac{1}{2} + \frac{7}{5} = \boxed{2\frac{9}{10}}$ Method 1: Convert the improper fraction to a mixed number.

> One denominator is not a multiple of the other. So, we need to express both fractions in tenths.

> 7 **divided into groups** of 5 is equal to 1 group, with 2 remaining, which gives $1\frac{2}{5}$.

$1\frac{1}{2} + 1\frac{2}{5} =$

$\frac{1}{2} = \frac{5}{10}$ $\frac{2}{5} = \frac{4}{10}$

$7 \div 5 = 1 \text{ r } 2$ $\frac{7}{5} = 1\frac{2}{5}$ $1\frac{1}{2} + 1\frac{2}{5} = 1\frac{5}{10} + 1\frac{4}{10} = \boxed{2\frac{9}{10}}$

> **Combine** the **whole** and fraction parts.

Method 2: Convert the mixed number to an improper fraction.

> There is 1 group of $\frac{2}{2}$. ($1 \times 2 = 2$)

> There is 1 half more. ($2 + 1 = 3$)

$1\frac{1}{2} = \frac{3}{2}$

$\frac{2}{2} + \frac{1}{2} = \frac{3}{2}$

$\frac{3}{2} + \frac{7}{5} =$

$\frac{3}{2} = \frac{15}{10}$ $\frac{7}{5} = \frac{14}{10}$

> Express both fractions in tenths.

$\frac{3}{2} + \frac{7}{5} = \frac{15}{10} + \frac{14}{10} = \frac{29}{10} = \boxed{2\frac{9}{10}}$

> Convert $\frac{29}{10}$ to the mixed number $2\frac{9}{10}$.

Add a proper fraction to a mixed number

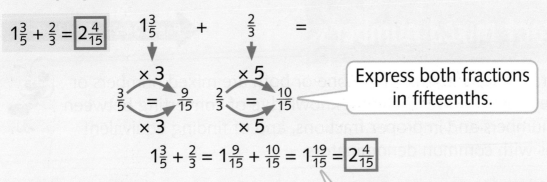

$$1\frac{3}{5} + \frac{2}{3} = \boxed{2\frac{4}{15}} \qquad 1\frac{3}{5} \quad + \quad \frac{2}{3} \quad =$$

$$\times 3 \qquad \times 5$$

$$\frac{3}{5} = \frac{9}{15} \qquad \frac{2}{3} = \frac{10}{15}$$

Express both fractions in fifteenths.

$$\times 3 \qquad \times 5$$

$$1\frac{3}{5} + \frac{2}{3} = 1\frac{9}{15} + \frac{10}{15} = 1\frac{19}{15} = \boxed{2\frac{4}{15}}$$

How else could you solve this fraction addition?

Convert $\frac{19}{15}$ to the mixed number $1\frac{4}{15}$ $(1 + 1\frac{4}{15} = 2\frac{4}{15})$

Add two mixed numbers

$$1\frac{2}{3} + 2\frac{3}{4} = \boxed{4\frac{5}{12}}$$

Method 1: Add the whole numbers then add the fractions.

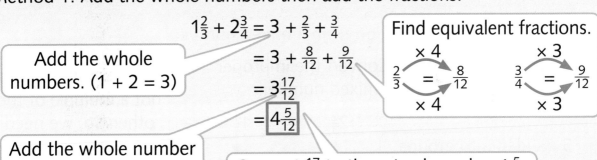

$$1\frac{2}{3} + 2\frac{3}{4} = 3 + \frac{2}{3} + \frac{3}{4}$$

Add the whole numbers. $(1 + 2 = 3)$

$$= 3 + \frac{8}{12} + \frac{9}{12}$$

$$= 3\frac{17}{12}$$

$$= \boxed{4\frac{5}{12}}$$

Find equivalent fractions.

$$\times 4 \qquad \times 3$$

$$\frac{2}{3} = \frac{8}{12} \qquad \frac{3}{4} = \frac{9}{12}$$

$$\times 4 \qquad \times 3$$

Add the whole number and the fractions. $(\frac{8}{12} + \frac{9}{12} = \frac{17}{12})$

Convert $\frac{17}{12}$ to the mixed number $1\frac{5}{12}$. $(3 + 1\frac{5}{12} = 4\frac{5}{12})$

Method 2: Convert both mixed numbers to improper fractions.

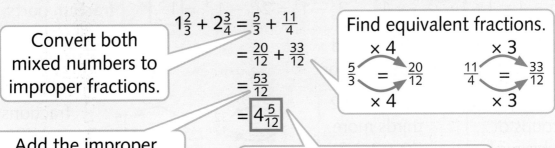

$$1\frac{2}{3} + 2\frac{3}{4} = \frac{5}{3} + \frac{11}{4}$$

Convert both mixed numbers to improper fractions.

$$= \frac{20}{12} + \frac{33}{12}$$

$$= \frac{53}{12}$$

$$= \boxed{4\frac{5}{12}}$$

Find equivalent fractions.

$$\times 4 \qquad \times 3$$

$$\frac{5}{3} = \frac{20}{12} \qquad \frac{11}{4} = \frac{33}{12}$$

$$\times 4 \qquad \times 3$$

Add the improper fractions with a common denominator.

Convert the improper fraction to a mixed number.

Pages 50-53

Subtract mixed numbers

Pages 24-25, 40-43, 46-47

To subtract two fractions where one or both are mixed numbers or improper fractions, we apply our knowledge of converting between mixed numbers and improper fractions, and of finding equivalent fractions with common denominators.

Subtract two improper fractions

$$\frac{5}{4} - \frac{6}{5} =$$

$$\frac{5}{4} - \frac{6}{5} = \boxed{\frac{1}{20}}$$

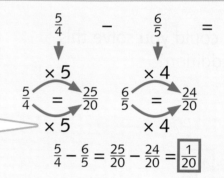

One **denominator** is not a **multiple** of the other. So, we need to **express** both **fractions** in twentieths.

$$\frac{5}{4} \xrightarrow{\times 5} \frac{25}{20} \qquad \frac{6}{5} \xrightarrow{\times 4} \frac{24}{20}$$

$$\frac{5}{4} - \frac{6}{5} = \frac{25}{20} - \frac{24}{20} = \boxed{\frac{1}{20}}$$

How else could you solve this fraction subtraction?

Subtract an improper fraction from a mixed number

$$2\frac{2}{3} - \frac{5}{4} = \boxed{1\frac{5}{12}}$$

Method 1: Convert the improper fraction to a mixed number.

One denominator is not a multiple of the other. So, we need to express both fractions in twelfths.

$$2\frac{2}{3} - 1\frac{1}{4} =$$

5 divided into groups of 4 is equal to 1 group, with 1 remaining, which gives $1\frac{1}{4}$.

$$\frac{2}{3} \xrightarrow{\times 4} \frac{8}{12} \qquad \frac{1}{4} \xrightarrow{\times 3} \frac{3}{12}$$

$$5 \div 4 = 1 \text{ r } 1 \qquad \frac{5}{4} = 1\frac{1}{4}$$

Subtract the **whole** and **fraction parts.**

$$2\frac{2}{3} - 1\frac{1}{4} = 2\frac{8}{12} - 1\frac{3}{12} = \boxed{1\frac{5}{12}}$$

Method 2: Convert the mixed number to an improper fraction.

$$\frac{8}{3} - \frac{5}{4} =$$

There are 2 groups of $\frac{3}{3}$, which is $\frac{6}{3}$. ($2 \times 3 = 6$)

There are 2 thirds more. ($6 + 2 = 8$)

Express both fractions in twelfths.

$$2\frac{2}{3} = \frac{8}{3}$$

$$\frac{6}{3} + \frac{2}{3} = \frac{8}{3}$$

$$\frac{8}{3} \xrightarrow{\times 4} \frac{32}{12} \qquad \frac{5}{4} \xrightarrow{\times 3} \frac{15}{12}$$

$$\frac{8}{3} - \frac{5}{4} = \frac{32}{12} - \frac{15}{12} = \frac{17}{12} = \boxed{1\frac{5}{12}}$$

Convert $\frac{17}{12}$ to the mixed number $1\frac{5}{12}$.

Subtract a proper fraction from a mixed number

$$3\frac{4}{5} - \frac{3}{4} = \boxed{3\frac{1}{20}}$$

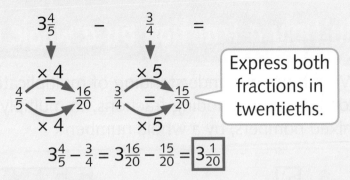

Express both fractions in twentieths.

$$3\frac{4}{5} - \frac{3}{4} = 3\frac{16}{20} - \frac{15}{20} = \boxed{3\frac{1}{20}}$$

How else could you solve this fraction subtraction?

Subtract two mixed numbers

$$3\frac{1}{5} - 1\frac{2}{3} = \boxed{1\frac{8}{15}}$$

Method 1: Subtract the whole numbers then subtract the fractions.

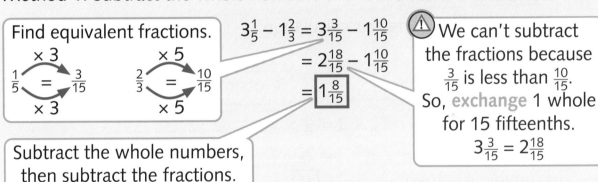

Find equivalent fractions.

$$3\frac{1}{5} - 1\frac{2}{3} = 3\frac{3}{15} - 1\frac{10}{15}$$
$$= 2\frac{18}{15} - 1\frac{10}{15}$$
$$= \boxed{1\frac{8}{15}}$$

Subtract the whole numbers, then subtract the fractions.

⚠ We can't subtract the fractions because $\frac{3}{15}$ is less than $\frac{10}{15}$. So, **exchange** 1 whole for 15 fifteenths.
$$3\frac{3}{15} = 2\frac{18}{15}$$

Method 2: Convert both mixed numbers to improper fractions.

Convert both mixed numbers to improper fractions.

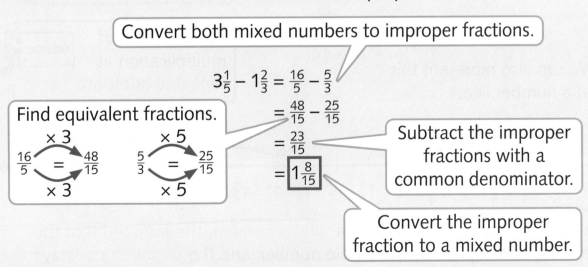

Find equivalent fractions.

$$3\frac{1}{5} - 1\frac{2}{3} = \frac{16}{5} - \frac{5}{3}$$
$$= \frac{48}{15} - \frac{25}{15}$$
$$= \frac{23}{15}$$
$$= \boxed{1\frac{8}{15}}$$

Subtract the improper fractions with a common denominator.

Convert the improper fraction to a mixed number.

Multiply a fraction by a whole number

Pages 40-41, 46-49

We can use our understanding of multiplication as repeated addition, and of adding fractions, to multiply a fraction, including mixed numbers, by a whole number.

$\frac{5}{6} \times 3 = \boxed{2\frac{1}{2}}$

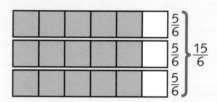

Look at this model.

There are 3 wholes.

Each **whole** has been **divided into** 6 **equal parts**, and 5 parts of each whole are shaded.

There are 15 sixths shaded **altogether**.

We can represent this using this calculation:

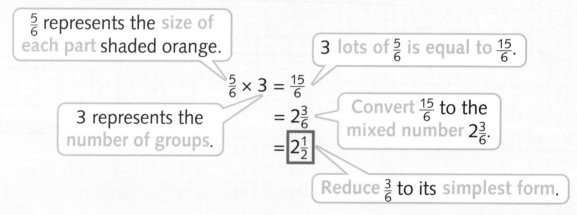

$\frac{5}{6}$ represents the **size of each part** shaded orange.

3 lots of $\frac{5}{6}$ is equal to $\frac{15}{6}$.

$\frac{5}{6} \times 3 = \frac{15}{6}$

3 represents the **number of groups**.

$= 2\frac{3}{6}$

Convert $\frac{15}{6}$ to the mixed number $2\frac{3}{6}$.

$= \boxed{2\frac{1}{2}}$

Reduce $\frac{3}{6}$ to its **simplest form**.

We can think of multiplication as **repeated addition**.

Remember

We can also represent this on a number line.

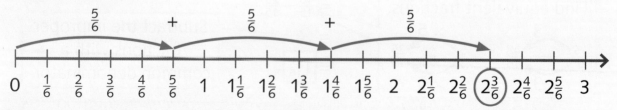

When multiplying a fraction by a **whole number**, the **numerator** of the **fraction** is multiplied by the whole number, and the **denominator** stays the same.

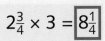
$2\frac{3}{4} \times 3 = \boxed{8\frac{1}{4}}$

Look at this model.

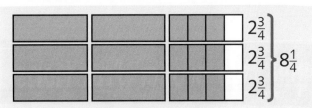

There are 3 groups, and each group has 2 wholes and 3 quarters shaded.

There are 6 wholes and 9 quarters shaded altogether.

9 quarters ($\frac{9}{4}$) is equal to 2 wholes and 1 quarter ($2\frac{1}{4}$), so 6 add $2\frac{1}{4}$ equals $8\frac{1}{4}$.

We can represent this using this calculation:

| $2\frac{3}{4}$ represents the size of each part shaded orange. | $2\frac{3}{4} \times 3 = \boxed{8\frac{1}{4}}$ | 3 lots of $2\frac{3}{4}$ is equal to $8\frac{1}{4}$. |

3 represents the number of groups.

We can work out this calculation using different methods.

Method 1: Repeated addition.

3 lots of $2\frac{3}{4}$ is equal to 3 lots of 2 wholes and 3 lots of $\frac{3}{4}$.

$2\frac{3}{4} \times 3 = 2\frac{3}{4} + 2\frac{3}{4} + 2\frac{3}{4}$
$= 6\frac{9}{4}$
$= \boxed{8\frac{1}{4}}$

Convert the improper fraction $\frac{9}{4}$ to the mixed number $2\frac{1}{4}$. ($6 + 2\frac{1}{4} = 8\frac{1}{4}$)

Method 2: Partition, then multiply the whole number and then the fraction.

Multiply the whole number by 3. ($2 \times 3 = 6$)

$2\frac{3}{4} \times 3 =$

Multiply the fraction by 3. ($\frac{3}{4} \times 3 = \frac{9}{4}$)

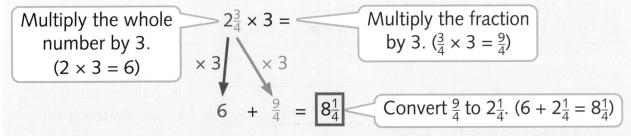

$\times 3$ $\times 3$

$6 \quad + \quad \frac{9}{4} \quad = \quad \boxed{8\frac{1}{4}}$

Convert $\frac{9}{4}$ to $2\frac{1}{4}$. ($6 + 2\frac{1}{4} = 8\frac{1}{4}$)

Method 3: Convert the mixed number to an improper fraction.

Convert $2\frac{3}{4}$ to $\frac{11}{4}$.

$2\frac{3}{4} \times 3 = \frac{11}{4} \times 3$
$\quad = \frac{33}{4}$
$\quad = \boxed{8\frac{1}{4}}$

Multiply the improper fraction by the whole number.

Convert $\frac{33}{4}$ to $8\frac{1}{4}$.

What's similar about each of these three methods?

What's different?

Which method do you prefer? Why?

Pages 54-55

Multiply two proper fractions

Pages 40–41, 52–53

When a fraction is multiplied by a proper fraction, it makes it smaller. To multiply two fractions, we multiply the numerators and multiply the denominators.

$$\frac{1}{2} \times \frac{1}{4} = \boxed{\frac{1}{8}}$$

When we multiply two fractions, it's helpful to think of the multiplication symbol (×) as meaning 'of'.

So, $\frac{1}{2} \times \frac{1}{4}$ is the same as $\frac{1}{2}$ of $\frac{1}{4}$.

Look at these models.

$\frac{1}{4}$ of the whole is shaded orange.

To find $\frac{1}{2}$ of the shaded $\frac{1}{4}$, the quarter has been divided into 2 equal parts.

1			
$\frac{1}{4}$	$\frac{1}{4}$	$\frac{1}{4}$	$\frac{1}{4}$

Each of the 4 parts has been divided into halves. So, there are 8 equal parts of that size altogether in the whole.

1			
$\frac{1}{4}$	$\frac{1}{4}$	$\frac{1}{4}$	$\frac{1}{4}$

The green part is $\frac{1}{8}$ of the whole.
So, $\frac{1}{2} \times \frac{1}{4} = \frac{1}{8}$.

1			
$\frac{1}{4}$	$\frac{1}{4}$	$\frac{1}{4}$	$\frac{1}{4}$
$\frac{1}{8}$ $\frac{1}{8}$	$\frac{1}{8}$ $\frac{1}{8}$	$\frac{1}{8}$ $\frac{1}{8}$	$\frac{1}{8}$ $\frac{1}{8}$

In halving each part, we doubled the number of parts. So, the denominator has doubled.

So, 1 half of 1 quarter is 1 eighth.

$\frac{1}{2}$ of $\frac{1}{4}$ is equal to $\frac{1}{8}$.

$\frac{1}{2}$ of $\frac{1}{4} = \frac{1}{8}$

or

$\frac{1}{2} \times \frac{1}{4} = \frac{1}{8}$

When multiplying unit fractions, the product is smaller than the fractions being multiplied.

So, $\frac{1}{2} \times \frac{1}{4} = \frac{1}{8}$ and $\frac{1}{4} \times \frac{1}{2} = \frac{1}{8}$.

Multiplication is commutative – it can be done in any order. Remember

$\frac{1}{2}$ of the whole is shaded orange.

The green part is $\frac{1}{8}$ of the whole. So, $\frac{1}{4} \times \frac{1}{2} = \frac{1}{8}$.

1
$\frac{1}{2}$	$\frac{1}{2}$

1
$\frac{1}{2}$	$\frac{1}{2}$

1
$\frac{1}{2}$	$\frac{1}{2}$
$\frac{1}{8}$	$\frac{1}{8}$	$\frac{1}{8}$	$\frac{1}{8}$	$\frac{1}{8}$	$\frac{1}{8}$	$\frac{1}{8}$	$\frac{1}{8}$

To find $\frac{1}{4}$ of the shaded $\frac{1}{2}$, the half has been divided into 4 equal parts.

Each of the 2 parts has been divided into quarters. So, there are 8 equal parts of that size altogether in the whole.

RULE: When we multiply unit fractions, we multiply the denominators.

What about multiplying non-unit fractions?

 $\frac{3}{4} \times \frac{1}{3} = \boxed{\frac{1}{4}}$

$\frac{1}{3}$ of the whole is shaded orange. To find $\frac{3}{4}$ of the shaded $\frac{1}{3}$, the third has been divided into 4 equal parts.

1
$\frac{1}{3}$	$\frac{1}{3}$	$\frac{1}{3}$

Each of the 3 parts has been divided into quarters. So, there are 12 equal parts of that size altogether in the whole.

1
$\frac{1}{3}$	$\frac{1}{3}$	$\frac{1}{3}$

The green parts are $\frac{3}{12}$ of the whole. So, $\frac{3}{4} \times \frac{1}{3} = \frac{3}{12}$.

We reduce $\frac{3}{12}$ to $\frac{1}{4}$. So $\frac{3}{4} \times \frac{1}{3} = \frac{1}{4}$.

1
$\frac{1}{3}$	$\frac{1}{3}$	$\frac{1}{3}$
$\frac{1}{12}$	$\frac{1}{12}$	$\frac{1}{12}$	$\frac{1}{12}$	$\frac{1}{12}$	$\frac{1}{12}$	$\frac{1}{12}$	$\frac{1}{12}$	$\frac{1}{12}$	$\frac{1}{12}$	$\frac{1}{12}$	$\frac{1}{12}$
$\frac{1}{4}$	$\frac{1}{4}$	$\frac{1}{4}$	$\frac{1}{4}$

Multiplication is commutative. So, $\frac{3}{4} \times \frac{1}{3} = \frac{3}{12} = \frac{1}{4}$ and $\frac{1}{3} \times \frac{3}{4} = \frac{3}{12} = \frac{1}{4}$.

RULE: When multiplying non-unit fractions, we multiply the numerators and we multiply the denominators.

$$\frac{3}{4} \times \frac{1}{3} = \frac{3}{12} = \frac{1}{4}$$

Pages 56-57

Divide a proper fraction by a whole number

Pages 40–41, 54–55

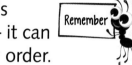

When a fraction is divided by a whole number, it makes the fraction smaller.

On pages 54 and 55, we saw that finding half of $\frac{1}{4}$ can be expressed as:

$\frac{1}{2} \times \frac{1}{4} = \frac{1}{8}$ and $\frac{1}{4} \times \frac{1}{2} = \frac{1}{8}$.

We can express this in another way:

Multiplication is commutative – it can be done in any order.

Remember

$\frac{1}{4} \div 2 = \boxed{\frac{1}{8}}$

$\frac{1}{4}$ of the whole is shaded orange.

1			
$\frac{1}{4}$	$\frac{1}{4}$	$\frac{1}{4}$	$\frac{1}{4}$

The quarter has been divided into 2 equal parts.

Each of the 4 quarters has been divided by 2. So, there are 8 equal parts altogether in the whole.

The green part is $\frac{1}{8}$ of the whole. So, $\frac{1}{4} \div 2 = \frac{1}{8}$.

So, $\frac{1}{4} \times \frac{1}{2} = \frac{1}{4} \div 2 = \frac{1}{8}$ — $\frac{1}{4}$ halved is the same as $\frac{1}{4} \div 2$.

What's the same about $\frac{1}{4} \times \frac{1}{2} = \frac{1}{8}$ and $\frac{1}{4} \div 2 = \frac{1}{8}$?
What's different?

Dividing by 2 is the same as multiplying by $\frac{1}{2}$. — $\frac{1}{4} \div 2 = \frac{1}{8} \rightarrow \frac{1}{4} \times \frac{1}{2} = \frac{1}{8}$

Therefore:

- dividing by 3 is the same as multiplying by $\frac{1}{3}$ — $\frac{1}{5} \div 3 = \frac{1}{15} \rightarrow \frac{1}{5} \times \frac{1}{3} = \frac{1}{15}$
- dividing by 5 is the same as multiplying by $\frac{1}{5}$. — $\frac{1}{2} \div 5 = \frac{1}{10} \rightarrow \frac{1}{2} \times \frac{1}{5} = \frac{1}{10}$

Let's look again at: $\frac{1}{4} \div 2 = \frac{1}{8}$

To divide a fraction by a whole number, we can change it to an equivalent multiplication.
So, to divide by 2, we can multiply by $\frac{1}{2}$.

1			
$\frac{1}{4}$	$\frac{1}{4}$	$\frac{1}{4}$	$\frac{1}{4}$

$\frac{1}{8}$	$\frac{1}{8}$	$\frac{1}{8}$	$\frac{1}{8}$	$\frac{1}{8}$	$\frac{1}{8}$	$\frac{1}{8}$	$\frac{1}{8}$

Now let's look at these calculations:

$\frac{1}{3} \div 4 = \boxed{\frac{1}{12}}$

To divide by 4, multiply by $\frac{1}{4}$. $\frac{1}{3} \times \frac{1}{4} = \frac{1}{12}$

$\frac{1}{7} \div 3 = \boxed{\frac{1}{21}}$

To divide by 3, multiply by $\frac{1}{3}$. $\frac{1}{7} \times \frac{1}{3} = \frac{1}{21}$

What about dividing non-unit fractions by a whole number?

$\frac{3}{4} \div 3 = \boxed{\frac{1}{4}}$

To divide by 3, multiply by $\frac{1}{3}$. $\frac{3}{4} \times \frac{1}{3} = \frac{3}{12}$

So, $\frac{3}{4} \div 3 = \frac{3}{4} \times \frac{1}{3} = \frac{3}{12} = \frac{1}{4}$

$\frac{2}{3} \div 5 = \boxed{\frac{2}{15}}$

To divide by 5, multiply by $\frac{1}{5}$. $\frac{2}{3} \times \frac{1}{5} = \frac{2}{15}$

So, $\frac{2}{3} \div 5 = \frac{2}{3} \times \frac{1}{5} = \frac{2}{15}$

$\frac{7}{8} \div 2 = \boxed{\frac{7}{16}}$

To divide by 2, multiply by $\frac{1}{2}$. $\frac{7}{8} \times \frac{1}{2} = \frac{7}{16}$

So, $\frac{7}{8} \div 2 = \frac{7}{8} \times \frac{1}{2} = \frac{7}{16}$

57

Fractions

Calculate a fraction of an amount

Pages 28-29
34-37, 40-41

We can find a fraction of an amount by dividing the whole by the denominator and multiplying the quotient by the numerator.

$\frac{1}{12}$ of 228 = 19

To calculate a unit fraction of an amount:

1. Find the total amount – the whole.

2. Divide the whole by the denominator.

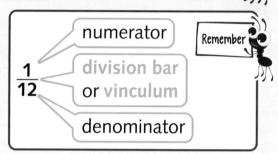

We can show this in a diagram.

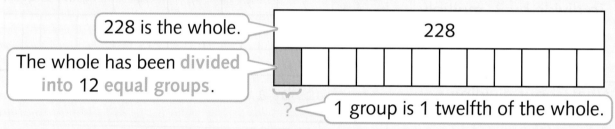

228 is the whole.

The whole has been divided into 12 equal groups.

228

? — 1 group is 1 twelfth of the whole.

When calculating a fraction of an amount, the denominator of the fraction tells us how many equal groups the whole is divided into.

The numerator of the fraction tells us how many groups of the whole we are finding.

Divide the whole by the denominator. — $\frac{1}{12}$ — Find the amount in 1 of the groups.

So, to find $\frac{1}{12}$ of 228:

Divide 228 by 12. — $228 \div 12 = 19$

We can say: — 228 divided into 12 equal groups is equal to 19.

We can also say: — 1 twelfth of 228 is equal to 19.

You could work out the division like this. How else might you work it out?

$$
\begin{array}{r}
0\ 1\ 9 \\
1\,2\overline{)2\ 2\ 8} \\
-\ 1\ 2 \downarrow \\
\hline
1\ 0\ 8 \\
-\ 1\ 0\ 8 \\
\hline
0
\end{array}
$$

 Draw Calculate:

$\frac{1}{7}$ of 252 = ☐ $\frac{1}{15}$ of 360 = ☐ $\frac{1}{30}$ of 4,800 = ☐

58

$\frac{7}{9}$ of 378 = 294

The **quotient** is the answer to a division calculation.

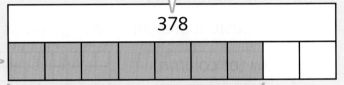

To calculate a **non-unit** fraction of an amount:

1. Find the total amount – the whole.

2. Divide the whole by the denominator.

3. Multiply the quotient by the numerator.

We can show this in a diagram.

378 is the whole.

378

The whole has been divided into 9 equal groups.

7 groups is 7 ninths of the whole.

?

Remember

When calculating a fraction of an amount, the denominator of the fraction tells us how many equal groups the whole is divided into.

The numerator of the fraction tells us how many groups of the whole we are finding.

Divide the whole by the denominator.

$\frac{7}{9}$

Find the amount in 7 of the groups.

So, to find $\frac{7}{9}$ of 378:

- divide 378 by 9 — $378 \div 9 = 42$

- then multiply the quotient by 7 to find the answer. — $42 \times 7 = 294$

We can say: — 378 divided into 9 equal groups is equal to 42, and 7 groups of 42 equals 294.

We can also say: — 7 ninths of 378 is equal to 294.

You could work out the division like this. How else might you work it out?

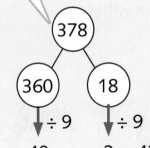

378

360   18

$\div 9$ $\div 9$

40 + 2 = 42

Draw

Calculate:

$\frac{3}{5}$ of 875 = ☐

$\frac{5}{12}$ of 468 = ☐

$\frac{7}{20}$ of 9,600 = ☐

Tenths, hundredths and thousandths

Decimal numbers consist of whole numbers and fractions of numbers. We can apply our understanding of place value to partition decimals in different ways.

Tenths and hundredths

This 100 square represents 1 **whole**. It has been divided into 100 **equal parts**.

Each row (or column) is 1 out of 10 equal rows (or columns). This row is 1 **tenth**. As a **fraction**, we write this as $\frac{1}{10}$. As a **decimal**, we write this as 0·1. We can also see that: $\frac{1}{10} = \frac{10}{100}$

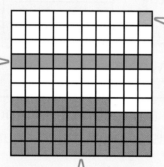

Each square is 1 out of 100 equal squares. This square is 1 **hundredth**. As a fraction, we write this as $\frac{1}{100}$. As a decimal, we write this as 0·01.

There are 37 green squares. So, 37 **hundredths** are shaded green. As a fraction, we write this as $\frac{37}{100}$. As a decimal, we write this as 0·37.

We can **decompose** or **partition tenths** and **hundredths** to show the place value of each digit.

We can also decompose or **regroup** decimals in other ways.

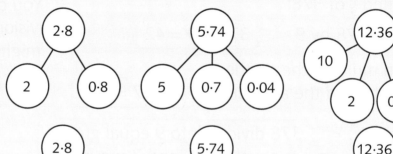

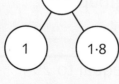

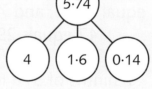

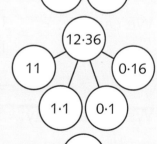

How else could you regroup each of these three decimals?

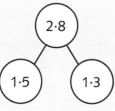

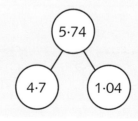

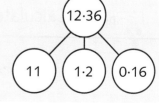

60

Thousandths

This 1,000 square represents 1 whole. It has been divided into 1,000 equal parts.

Each part is 1 out of 1,000 equal parts. This red part is 1 thousandth. As a fraction, we write this as $\frac{1}{1,000}$. As a decimal, we write this as 0·001.

There are 100 green parts. So, 100 thousandths are shaded green. As a fraction, we write this as $\frac{100}{1,000}$. As a decimal, we write this as 0·1. We can also see that:
$$\frac{100}{1,000} = \frac{1}{10}$$

There are 10 blue parts. So, 10 thousandths are shaded blue. As a fraction, we write this as $\frac{10}{1,000}$. As a decimal, we write this as 0·01. We can also see that:
$$\frac{10}{1,000} = \frac{1}{100}$$

There are 476 orange parts. So, 476 thousandths are shaded orange. As a fraction, we write this as $\frac{476}{1,000}$. As a decimal, we write this as 0·476.

We can partition thousandths to show the place value of each digit and also regroup them in other ways.

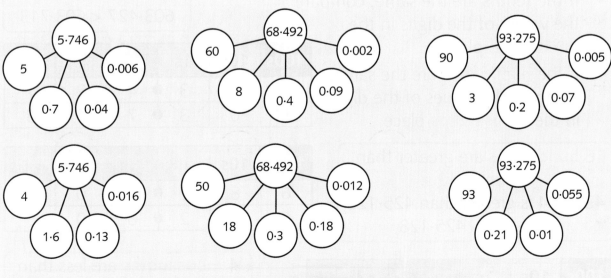

  How else could you regroup each of these three decimals?

Pages 62-93

Compare and order decimals

Pages 10-11, 60-61

Just like with whole numbers, when we compare decimals we use language such as greater/smaller than, and more/less than and the inequality symbols > and <.

> — greater than | Remember

< — less than

---

2 **hundreds** has the greatest place value.

100s	10s	1s	$\frac{1}{10}$s	$\frac{1}{100}$s	$\frac{1}{1,000}$s
2	6	3	4	5	8

8 thousandths has the smallest place value.

Look at each pair of decimals below.
Compare the digits in the place value columns from left to right.

- Start by comparing the whole numbers.
- If the whole numbers are the same, compare the values of the digits in the tenths place.
- If the tenths are the same, compare the values of the digits in the hundredths place.
- If the hundredths are the same, compare the values of the digits in the thousandths place.

4 **tenths** are less than 7 **tenths**.
603·427 is less than 603·713
603·427 < 603·713

100s	10s	1s	$\frac{1}{10}$s	$\frac{1}{100}$s	$\frac{1}{1,000}$s
6	0	3	4	2	7
6	0	3	7	1	3

6 hundredths are greater than 2 hundredths.
425·164 is greater than 425·128
425·164 > 425·128

100s	10s	1s	$\frac{1}{10}$s	$\frac{1}{100}$s	$\frac{1}{1,000}$s
6	8	2	6	0	4
6	8	2	6	0	9

100s	10s	1s	$\frac{1}{10}$s	$\frac{1}{100}$s	$\frac{1}{1,000}$s
4	2	5	1	6	4
4	2	5	1	2	8

4 thousandths are less than 9 thousandths.
682·604 is less than 682·609
682·604 < 682·609

We can **order** a set of decimal numbers:
in **ascending** order – from **smallest** to **largest/greatest**
or in **descending** order – from largest/greatest to smallest.

Like when we compare decimals, when we order decimals, we start with the digits with the greatest place value. If the digits with the greatest place value are the same, we look at the place value columns to the right until they are different digits.

Descending order – largest to smallest

> If the whole numbers are the same, compare the values of the digits in the **tenths** place.

> Start by comparing whole numbers.

100s	10s	1s	$\frac{1}{10}$s	$\frac{1}{100}$s	$\frac{1}{1,000}$s
2	5	4	6	8	3
3	0	2	5	4	
3	0	2	9		
2	5	4	6	9	
2	5	4	6	8	9
3	0	2	5	4	1

> If the **tenths** are the same, compare the values of the digits in the **hundredths** place.

> If the **hundredths** are the same, compare the values of the digits in the **thousandths** place.

302·9 > 302·541 > 302·54 > 254·69 > 254·689 > 254·683

Ascending order – smallest to largest

| 28·403 | < | 28·504 | < | 28·51 | < | 28·6 | < | 28·601 |

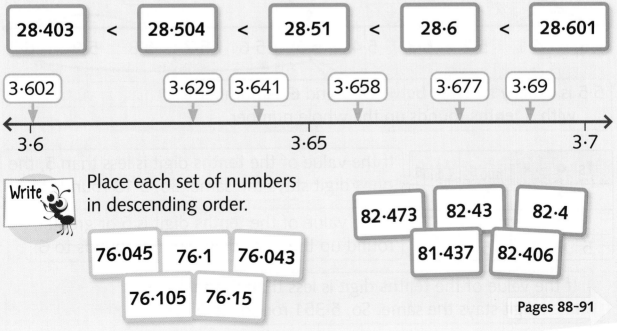

Write

Place each set of numbers in descending order.

76·045   76·1   76·043

76·105   76·15

82·473   82·43   82·4

81·437   82·406

Pages 88–91

Round decimals

Pages 12-13, 60-61

Rounding means changing a number to another number that is close to it in value. Rounding numbers often makes them easier to use. We round decimals in the same way as we round whole numbers.

Round decimals to the nearest whole number

We **round** decimals to the nearest **whole number**, depending on which whole number the decimal is closer to.

To round decimals to the nearest whole number, look at the **digit** in the **tenths place value**.

We can round **tenths**, **hundreds** and **thousandths** to the nearest whole number.

Look at these three decimals:

| 5·13 | 5·8 | 5·351 |

A number line is a useful tool to help with rounding.

5·13 is closer to 5 than to 6. So, the whole number **stays the same**: 5.

5·351 is closer to 5 than to 6. So, the whole number stays the same: 5.

5·8 is closer to 6 than to 5. So, **round up** the whole number to 6.

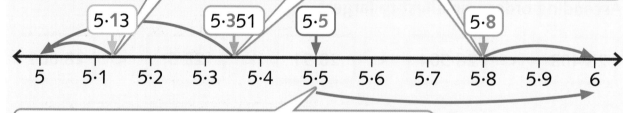

5·13   5·351   5·5   5·8

5   5·1   5·2   5·3   5·4   5·5   5·6   5·7   5·8   5·9   6

5·5 is exactly **halfway between** 5 and 6. A number with **5 tenths** rounds up the whole number.

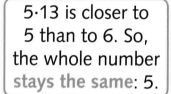

1s	$\frac{1}{10}$s	$\frac{1}{100}$s	$\frac{1}{1,000}$s
5	1	3	
5	8		
5	3	5	1

If the value of the **tenths** digit is less than 5, the **ones** digit stays the same. So, 5·13 rounds to 5.

If the value of the **tenths** digit is 5 or greater, round up the **ones** digit. So, 5·8 rounds to 6.

If the value of the **tenths** digit is less than 5, the **ones** digit stays the same. So, 5·351 rounds to 5.

Round decimals to the nearest tenth

As well as rounding decimals to the nearest whole number, we can round hundredths and thousandths to the nearest **tenth**.

To round decimals to the nearest **tenth**, look at the digit in the hundredths place value.

Look at these two decimals:

27·53   **27·584**

Once again, a number line is a useful tool to help with rounding.

> 27·53 is closer to 27·5 than to 27·6. So, the **tenths** digit stays the same: 27·5.

> 27·584 is closer to 27·6 than to 27·5. So, round up the **tenths** digit to 27·6.

27·53   27·55   27·584

27·5 27·51 27·52 27·53 27·54 27·55 27·56 27·57 27·58 27·59 27·6

> The rule for rounding a number with 5 hundredths is to round up the **tenths**.

10s	1s	$\frac{1}{10}$s	$\frac{1}{100}$s	$\frac{1}{1,000}$s
2	7	5	3	
2	7	5	8	4

> If the value of the hundredths digit is less than 5, the **tenths** digit stays the same. So, 27·53 rounds to 27·5.

> If the value of the hundredths digit is 5 or greater, round up the **tenths** digit. So, 27·584 rounds to 27·6.

Round decimals to the nearest hundredth

We can also round thousandths to the nearest hundredth.

To round decimals to the nearest hundredth, look at the digit in the thousandths place value.

Look at these three decimals:

4·824   **4·827**   **4·825**

1s	$\frac{1}{10}$s	$\frac{1}{100}$s	$\frac{1}{1,000}$s
4	8	2	4
4	8	2	7
4	8	2	5

> If the value of the thousandths digit is less than 5, the hundredths digit stays the same. So, 4·824 rounds to 4·82.

> If the value of the thousandths digit is 5 or greater, round up the hundredths digit. So, 4·827 rounds to 4·83, and 4·825 also rounds to 4·83.

Pages 70–75, 82–85

Use known facts to add and subtract decimals

Pages 18–19, 60–61

We can apply place value knowledge to known addition and subtraction facts to add and subtract tenths, hundredths and thousandths.

Remember

Addition can be done in any order – it's **commutative**.

Addition and subtraction are related. If we know one addition or subtraction fact, we know three other related facts (**fact families**).

We can use known facts to help work out addition and subtraction facts involving **tenths**, **hundredths** and **thousandths**.

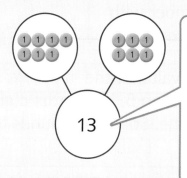

If we know that:
7 ones + 6 ones = 13 ones
$7 + 6 = 13$
We also know that:
$6 + 7 = 13$
$13 - 6 = 7$
$13 - 7 = 6$

Using known facts to add and subtract tenths

Change the **ones** to **tenths**.

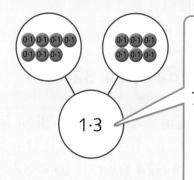

If we know that:
7 ones + 6 ones = 13 ones
we also know that:
7 tenths + 6 tenths = 13 tenths
$0.7 + 0.6 = 1.3$
and that:
$0.6 + 0.7 = 1.3$
$1.3 - 0.6 = 0.7$
$1.3 - 0.7 = 0.6$

Using known facts to add and subtract hundredths

Change the **ones** to **hundredths**.

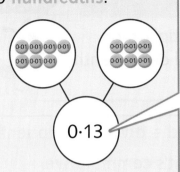

If we know that:
7 ones + 6 ones = 13 ones
we also know that:
7 hundredths + 6 hundredths = 13 hundredths
$0.07 + 0.06 = 0.13$
and that:
$0.06 + 0.07 = 0.13$
$0.13 - 0.06 = 0.07$
$0.13 - 0.07 = 0.06$

Using known facts to add and subtract thousandths

Change the **ones** to **thousandths**.

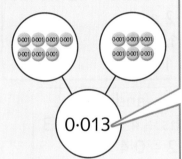

If we know that:
7 ones + 6 ones = 13 ones
we also know that:
7 thousandths + 6 thousandths = 13 thousandths
$0.007 + 0.006 = 0.013$
and that:
$0.006 + 0.007 = 0.013$
$0.013 - 0.006 = 0.007$
$0.013 - 0.007 = 0.006$

 Say

If you know that 9 + 3 = 12, what other addition and subtraction facts do you know?

 Work out the missing numbers.

$0.5 + \boxed{} = 0.8$ $0.17 - \boxed{} = 0.06$ $\boxed{} + 0.007 = 0.019$

$0.002 - \boxed{} = 0.005$ $0.08 + \boxed{} = 0.16$ $\boxed{} - 0.09 = 0.02$

$\boxed{} + 0.03 = 0.14$ $\boxed{} - 0.004 = 0.011$ $0.06 + \boxed{} = 0.07$

Pages 70-75

Use known facts to multiply and divide decimals

Pages 28-29, 60-61

We can apply place value knowledge to known multiplication tables facts and related division facts to multiply and divide tenths, hundredths and thousandths.

Remember
factor × factor = product   dividend ÷ divisor = quotient

Multiplication can be done in any order – it's commutative.

Multiplication and division are related. If we know one multiplication or division fact, we know three other related facts (fact families).

Using known facts to multiply and divide tenths

… we also know that: 3 × 4 tenths = 12 tenths
3 × 0·4 = 1·2 and
3 tenths × 4 = 12 tenths
0·3 × 4 = 1·2

If we know that:
3 × 4 = 12…

10 times smaller

… and:
12 tenths ÷ 4 tenths = 3
1·2 ÷ 0·4 = 3
12 tenths ÷ 4 = 3 tenths
1·2 ÷ 4 = 0·3

3 × 4 = 12	3 × 4 = 12	12 ÷ 4 = 3	12 ÷ 4 = 3
↓ ↓	↓ ↓	↓ ↓	↓ ↓
3 × 0·4 = 1·2	0·3 × 4 = 1·2	1·2 ÷ 0·4 = 3	1·2 ÷ 4 = 0·3

If one factor is 1 tenth of the size, the product will be 1 tenth of the size.

If the dividend is 1 tenth of the size and the divisor is 1 tenth of the size, the quotient remains the same.

If the dividend is 1 tenth of the size and the divisor remains the same, the quotient is 1 tenth of the size.

So,

3 × 4 = 12	and	3 × 0·4 = 1·2	and	0·3 × 4 = 1·2
4 × 3 = 12		0·4 × 3 = 1·2		4 × 0·3 = 1·2
12 ÷ 4 = 3		1·2 ÷ 0·4 = 3		1·2 ÷ 4 = 0·3
12 ÷ 3 = 4		1·2 ÷ 3 = 0·4		1·2 ÷ 0·3 = 4

Using known facts to multiply and divide hundredths

> … then: 3 × 4 **hundredths** = 12 **hundredths**
> 3 × 0·04 = 0·12 and
> 3 **hundredths** × 4 = 12 **hundredths**
> 0·03 × 4 = 0·12

> If we know that:
> 3 × 4 = 12…

100 times smaller

> … and:
> 12 **hundredths** ÷ 4 **hundredths** = 3
> 0·12 ÷ 0·04 = 3
> 12 **hundredths** ÷ 4 = 3 **hundredths**
> 0·12 ÷ 4 = 0·03

$$3 × 4 = 12 \qquad 3 × 4 = 12 \qquad 12 ÷ 4 = 3 \qquad 12 ÷ 4 = 3$$

$$3 × 0·04 = 0·12 \qquad 0·03 × 4 = 0·12 \qquad 0·12 ÷ 0·04 = 3 \qquad 0·12 ÷ 4 = 0·03$$

> If one factor is 1 **hundredth** of the size, the product will be 1 **hundredth** of the size.

> If the dividend is 1 **hundredth** of the size and the divisor is 1 **hundredth** of the size, the quotient remains the same.

> If the dividend is 1 **hundredth** of the size and the divisor remains the same, the quotient is 1 **hundredth** of the size.

So,

3 × 4 = 12	3 × 0·04 = 0·12	0·03 × 4 = 0·12
4 × 3 = 12	0·04 × 3 = 0·12	4 × 0·03 = 0·12
12 ÷ 4 = 3	0·12 ÷ 0·04 = 3	0·12 ÷ 4 = 0·03
12 ÷ 3 = 4	0·12 ÷ 3 = 0·04	0·12 ÷ 0·03 = 4

with "and" between the first/second and second/third columns.

Using known facts to multiply and divide thousandths

> If we know that:
> 3 × 4 = 12…

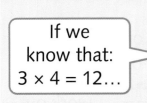

1,000 times smaller

> … then:
> 3 × 0·004 = 0·012
> 0·003 × 4 = 0·012
> 0·012 ÷ 0·004 = 3
> 0·012 ÷ 4 = 0·003

What other related multiplication and division facts do you know?

Pages 70–71, 82–85

Calculate mentally with decimals

Pages 18–23, 28–37, 60–61, 64–69

We can use known number facts, inverse relationships, properties of arithmetic, and place value knowledge to calculate mentally with decimals.

Remember

addend (or augend) + addend = sum (or total)
minuend − subtrahend = difference
factor × factor = product
dividend ÷ divisor = quotient

$+ \leftrightarrow -$
$\times \leftrightarrow \div$

⚠ **ALWAYS:**
Estimate
Calculate
Check

Addition and subtraction, and multiplication and division, are related – they are inverse operations.

We can use the following properties of arithmetic to solve calculations mentally:

$$0.5 + 0.7 = 0.7 + 0.5$$
$$0.4 \times 3 = 3 \times 0.4$$

- **commutative property** – changing the order of the addends or the factors does not change the sum or the product.

- **associative property** – changing the grouping of the addends or the factors does not change the sum or the product.

$$1.4 + 1.5 + 1.6 = 1.6 + 1.4 + 1.5$$
$$0.32 \times 5 = 0.4 \times 0.8 \times 5$$
$$= 0.4 \times 4$$
$$= 1.6$$

- **distributive property** – a multiplication calculation can be **partitioned** into the sum of two or more smaller calculations.

$$8 \times 6.4 = (8 \times 6) + (8 \times 0.4)$$
$$= 48 + 3.2$$
$$= 51.2$$

Understanding and applying **compensation properties** can also help us solve calculations involving decimals mentally.

Adding decimals

$$5.7 + 7.6 = \boxed{13.3}$$

Partition both numbers.
$$5.7 + 7.6 = 5 + 0.7 + 7 + 0.6$$
$$= 12 + 1.3$$
$$= 13.3$$

Partition one number.
$$5.7 + 7.6 = 5.7 + 7 + 0.6$$
$$= 12.7 + 0.6$$
$$= 13.3$$

$$6.5 + 0.78 = \boxed{7.28}$$

Use a number line (counting on).

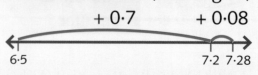

Use a compensation strategy.

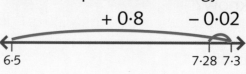

How else could you work out the answer to each of these additions?

Subtracting decimals

$8.3 - 4.7 = \boxed{3.6}$

Partition the subtrahend.
$8.3 - 4.7 = 8.3 - 4 - 0.7$
$ = 4.3 - 0.7$
$ = 3.6$

Use a known fact.
$83 - 47 = 36$
$8.3 - 4.7 = 3.6$ ⟶ 10 times smaller than $83 - 47 = 36$

$7.7 - 2.57 = \boxed{5.13}$

Use a number line (counting back).

$-0.07 \quad -0.5 \qquad -2$

5.13 5.2   5.7   7.7

Use a compensation strategy.
$7.7 - 2.57 = 5.13$
$+0.3 \downarrow \qquad \downarrow +0.3 \qquad =$
$8 - 2.87 = 5.13$

How else could you work out the answer to each of these subtractions?

Multiplying decimals

$5.6 \times 5 = \boxed{28}$

Use a compensation strategy.
$5.6 \times 5 = 28$
$\div 2 \downarrow \qquad \downarrow \times 2 \qquad =$
$2.8 \times 10 = 28$

$4.63 \times 3 = \boxed{13.89}$

Apply the distributive law.
$4.63 \times 3 = (4 \times 3) + (0.6 \times 3) + (0.03 \times 3)$
$ = 12 + 1.8 + 0.09$
$ = 13.89$

How else could you work out the answer to each of these multiplications?

Dividing decimals

$9.2 \div 4 = \boxed{2.3}$

Divide using the distributive law.

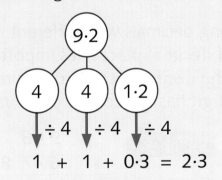

$1 \;+\; 1 \;+\; 0.3 \;=\; 2.3$

$34.6 \div 5 = \boxed{6.92}$

Use a compensation strategy.
$34.6 \div 5 = 6.92$
$\times 2 \downarrow \quad \div 2 \downarrow \qquad \times 2 =$
$34.6 \div 10 = 3.46$

How else could you work out the answer to each of these divisions?

For more on addition and subtraction compensation properties, see pages 18 and 19, and for multiplication and division compensation properties, see pages 28 and 29.

Pages 72–75, 82–85

Decimals

Add decimals with up to 3 decimal places

Pages 60-61, 64-67, 70-71

We can apply our understanding of adding whole numbers and of place value when we add decimals, including numbers with different numbers of decimal places.

$3·546 + 4·827 = \boxed{8·373}$

First **partition** both numbers into **ones**, **tenths**, hundredths and thousandths.

⚠ **ALWAYS:**
Estimate
Calculate
Check

Finally **combine** the thousandths, hundredths, **tenths** and ones.

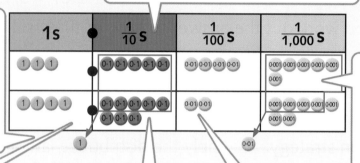

Then **add** the thousandths. As there are more than 10 thousandths, we need to **regroup** 10 thousandths into 1 hundredth.

Then add the ones.

Now add the **tenths**. As there are more than 10 **tenths**, we need to **regroup** 10 **tenths** into 1 one.

Next add the hundredths.

We can record this in columns.

```
  3 · 5 4 6
+ 4 · 8 2 7
─────────
      1 3
      6 0
  1 · 3 0 0
  7 · 0 0 0
─────────
  8 · 3 7 3
```

leads to

```
  3 · 5 4 6
+ 4 · 8 2 7
─────────
  8 · 3 7 3
    1     1
```

When adding decimals with different numbers of **decimal places**, it's important to line up the **decimal points** to ensure that each **digit** has the correct **place value**.

$9·6 + 6·78 = \boxed{16·38}$

Add the hundredths.

Add the **tenths**.

Add the ones.

```
    9 · 6
+   6 · 7 8
─────────
    0 · 0 8
    1 · 3 0
  1 5 · 0 0
─────────
  1 6 · 3 8
```

leads to

```
    9 · 6
+   6 · 7 8
─────────
  1 6 · 3 8
      1
```

Combine the hundredths, **tenths** and ones.

$5 \cdot 76 + 2 \cdot 985 = \boxed{8 \cdot 745}$

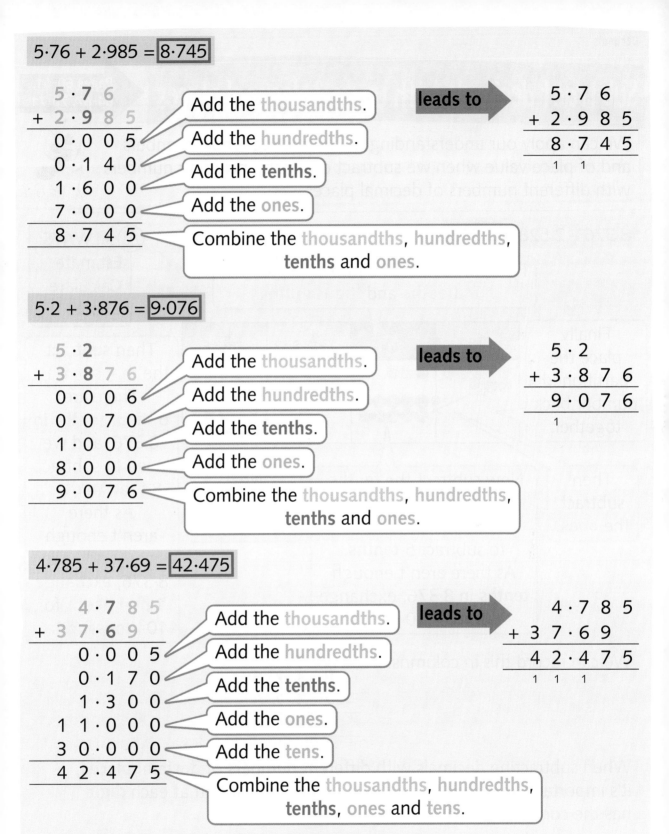

```
  5 · 7 6
+ 2 · 9 8 5
  0 · 0 0 5        Add the thousandths.
  0 · 1 4 0        Add the hundredths.
  1 · 6 0 0        Add the tenths.
  7 · 0 0 0        Add the ones.
  8 · 7 4 5        Combine the thousandths, hundredths,
                   tenths and ones.
```

leads to

```
  5 · 7 6
+ 2 · 9 8 5
  8 · 7 4 5
    1   1
```

$5 \cdot 2 + 3 \cdot 876 = \boxed{9 \cdot 076}$

```
  5 · 2
+ 3 · 8 7 6
  0 · 0 0 6        Add the thousandths.
  0 · 0 7 0        Add the hundredths.
  1 · 0 0 0        Add the tenths.
  8 · 0 0 0        Add the ones.
  9 · 0 7 6        Combine the thousandths, hundredths,
                   tenths and ones.
```

leads to

```
  5 · 2
+ 3 · 8 7 6
  9 · 0 7 6
    1
```

$4 \cdot 785 + 37 \cdot 69 = \boxed{42 \cdot 475}$

```
   4 · 7 8 5
+ 3 7 · 6 9
   0 · 0 0 5       Add the thousandths.
   0 · 1 7 0       Add the hundredths.
   1 · 3 0 0       Add the tenths.
 1 1 · 0 0 0       Add the ones.
 3 0 · 0 0 0       Add the tens.
 4 2 · 4 7 5       Combine the thousandths, hundredths,
                   tenths, ones and tens.
```

leads to

```
   4 · 7 8 5
+ 3 7 · 6 9
 4 2 · 4 7 5
   1   1   1
```

Look at the calculations on pages 72 and 73.

What other methods could you use to work out the answer to each calculation?

Which method do you prefer? Why?

Subtract decimals with up to 3 decimal places

Pages 60-61, 64-67, 70-71

We can apply our understanding of subtracting whole numbers and of place value when we subtract decimals, including numbers with different numbers of decimal places.

$8·376 – 2·528 = \boxed{5·848}$

⚠ **ALWAYS:**
Estimate
Calculate
Check

First **partition** 8·376 into ones, tenths, hundredths and thousandths.

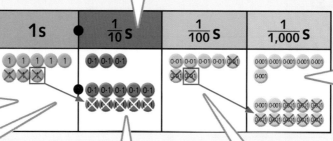

Finally place the partitioned number back together.

Then **subtract** the thousandths. There are 6 thousandths in 8·376, and we need to subtract 8 thousandths. As there aren't enough thousandths in 8·376, **exchange** 1 hundredth for 10 thousandths.

Then subtract the ones.

Now subtract the **tenths**. There are 3 **tenths** in 8·376, and we need to subtract 5 **tenths**. As there aren't enough **tenths** in 8·376, exchange 1 **one** for 10 **tenths**.

Next subtract the hundredths.

We can record this in columns.

$$\begin{array}{r} {}^{7}\!\!\not{8} \cdot {}^{13}\!\!\not{3} \; {}^{6}\!\!\not{7} \; {}^{16}\!\!\not{6} \\ -\; 2 \cdot 5 \;\; 2 \;\; 8 \\ \hline 5 \cdot 8 \;\; 4 \;\; 8 \end{array}$$

When subtracting decimals with different numbers of **decimal places**, it's important to line up the **decimal points** to ensure that each **digit** has the correct **place value**.

$9·52 – 6·7 = \boxed{2·82}$

$$\begin{array}{r} {}^{8}\!\!\not{9} \cdot {}^{15}\!\!\not{5} \; 2 \\ -\; 6 \cdot 7 \\ \hline 2 \cdot 8 \;\; 2 \end{array}$$

There are 5 **tenths** in 9·52, and we need to subtract 7 **tenths**. As there aren't enough **tenths** in 9·52, exchange 1 **one** for 10 **tenths**.

$6 \cdot 3 - 2 \cdot 87 = \boxed{3 \cdot 43}$

$$
\begin{array}{r}
\overset{5}{\cancel{6}} \cdot \overset{\overset{12}{\cancel{3}}}{} \overset{10}{} \\
- \ 2 \cdot 8 \ 7 \\
\hline
3 \cdot 4 \ 3 \\
\end{array}
$$

There are no hundredths in 6·3, and we need to subtract 7 hundredths. As there are no hundredths in 6·3, exchange 1 **tenth** for 10 hundredths.

After the exchange of 1 **tenth** for 10 hundredths there are now 2 **tenths**, and we need to subtract 8 **tenths**. As there aren't enough **tenths**, exchange 1 one for 10 **tenths**.

$36 \cdot 54 - 8 \cdot 798 = \boxed{27 \cdot 742}$

$$
\begin{array}{r}
\overset{2}{\cancel{3}} \ \overset{15}{\cancel{6}} \cdot \overset{14}{\cancel{5}} \ \overset{13}{\cancel{4}} \ \overset{10}{} \\
- \quad 8 \cdot 7 \ 9 \ 8 \\
\hline
2 \ 7 \cdot 7 \ 4 \ 2 \\
\end{array}
$$

There are no thousandths in 36·54, and we need to subtract 8 thousandths. As there are no thousandths in 36·54, exchange 1 hundredth for 10 thousandths.

There are 6 ones in 36·54, and we need to subtract 8 ones. As there aren't enough ones in 36·54, exchange 1 ten for 10 ones.

After the exchange of 1 hundredth for 10 thousandths there are now 3 hundredths, and we need to subtract 9 hundredths. As there aren't enough hundredths, exchange 1 **tenth** for 10 hundredths.

$54 \cdot 8 - 7 \cdot 263 = \boxed{47 \cdot 537}$

$$
\begin{array}{r}
\overset{4}{\cancel{5}} \ \overset{14}{\cancel{4}} \cdot \overset{7}{\cancel{8}} \overset{\overset{9}{10}}{} \ \overset{10}{} \\
- \quad 7 \cdot 2 \ 6 \ 3 \\
\hline
4 \ 7 \cdot 5 \ 3 \ 7 \\
\end{array}
$$

There are no thousandths in 54·8, and we need to subtract 3 thousandths. As there are no hundredths in 54·8, we can't exchange 1 hundredth for 10 thousandths. So we need to exchange 1 **tenth** for 10 hundredths, and then exchange 1 hundredth for 10 thousandths.

After the exchange of 1 **tenth** for 10 hundredths, and the exchange of 1 hundredth for 10 thousandths, there are now 7 **tenths** and 9 hundredths.

Look at the calculations on pages 74 and 75.

What other methods could you use to work out the answer to each calculation?

Which method do you prefer? Why?

Multiply whole numbers and decimals by 10, 100 and 1,000

Pages 60-61

It's important to understand what happens to the place value of the digits when you multiply whole numbers and decimals by 10, 100 or 1,000.

When you move up one row on a Gattegno chart, the number becomes 10 times greater. $0.2 \times 10 = 2$

When you move up two rows on a Gattegno chart, the number becomes 100 times greater. $0.5 \times 100 = 50$ $6 \times 100 = 600$

100	200	300	400	500	600	700	800	900
10	20	30	40	50	60	70	80	90
1	2	3	4	5	6	7	8	9
0·1	0·2	0·3	0·4	0·5	0·6	0·7	0·8	0·9
0·01	0·02	0·03	0·04	0·05	0·06	0·07	0·08	0·09
0·001	0·002	0·003	0·004	0·005	0·006	0·007	0·008	0·009

When you move up three rows on a Gattegno chart, the number becomes 1,000 times greater. $0.08 \times 1,000 = 80$

Multiplying by 10

When we multiply a whole number or a decimal by 10, the value of each digit in the number becomes 10 times greater and the digits move one place value to the left.

When multiplying a whole number by 10, include a zero in the ones place to act as a place holder.

10,000s	1,000s	100s	10s	1s
	5	6	4	8
5	6	4	8	0

$5,648 \times 10 = 56,480$

$165.439 \times 10 = 1,654.39$

100s	10s	1s	$\frac{1}{10}$s
	5	3	2
5	3	2	

$53.2 \times 10 = 532$

1,000s	100s	10s	1s	$\frac{1}{10}$s	$\frac{1}{100}$s	$\frac{1}{1,000}$s
		1	6	5	4	3	9
	1	6	5	4	3	9	

100	200	300	400	500	600	700	800	900
10	20	30	40	50	60	70	80	90
1	2	3	4	5	6	7	8	9
0·1	0·2	0·3	0·4	0·5	0·6	0·7	0·8	0·9
0·01	0·02	0·03	0·04	0·05	0·06	0·07	0·08	0·09

$24.69 \times 10 = 246.9$

Multiplying by 100

When we multiply whole numbers or decimals by 100, the value of each digit in the number becomes 100 times greater and the digits move two place values to the left.

100,000s	10,000s	1,000s	100s	10s	1s
		5	4	3	8
5	4	3	8	0	0

$5{,}438 \times 100 = 543{,}800$

Include zeros as place holders.

1,000	2,000	3,000	4,000	5,000	6,000	7,000	8,000	9,000
100	200	300	400	500	600	700	800	900
10	20	30	40	50	60	70	80	90
1	2	3	4	5	6	7	8	9
0·1	0·2	0·3	0·4	0·5	0·6	0·7	0·8	0·9
0·01	0·02	0·03	0·04	0·05	0·06	0·07	0·08	0·09

100s	10s	1s	$\frac{1}{10}$s
		7	5
7	5	0	

$7{\cdot}5 \times 100 = 750$

$25{\cdot}78 \times 100 = 2{,}578$

10,000s	1,000s	100s	10s	1s	$\frac{1}{10}$s	$\frac{1}{100}$s
		5	6	3	2	9
5	6	3	2	9		

$563{\cdot}29 \times 100 = 56{,}329$

Multiplying by 1,000

When we multiply whole numbers or decimals by 1,000, the value of each digit in the number becomes 1,000 times greater and the digits move three place values to the left.

1,000,000s	100,000s	10,000s	1,000s	100s	10s	1s
			7	5	4	1
7	5	4	1	0	0	0

$7{,}541 \times 1{,}000 = 7{,}541{,}000$

Include zeros as place holders.

10,000s	1,000s	100s	10s	1s	$\frac{1}{10}$s
			3	4	8
3	4	8	0	0	

$34{\cdot}8 \times 1{,}000 = 34{,}800$

1,000s	100s	10s	1s	$\frac{1}{10}$s	$\frac{1}{100}$s	$\frac{1}{1,000}$s
			9	4	1	2
9	4	1	2			

$9{\cdot}412 \times 1{,}000 = 9{,}412$

1,000	2,000	3,000	4,000	5,000	6,000	7,000	8,000	9,000
100	200	300	400	500	600	700	800	900
10	20	30	40	50	60	70	80	90
1	2	3	4	5	6	7	8	9
0·1	0·2	0·3	0·4	0·5	0·6	0·7	0·8	0·9
0·01	0·02	0·03	0·04	0·05	0·06	0·07	0·08	0·09

$1{\cdot}46 \times 1{,}000 = 1{,}460$

Pages 78-79, 82-83

Divide whole numbers and decimals by 10, 100 and 1,000

Pages 60-61, 76-77

It's important to understand what happens to the place value of the digits when you divide whole numbers and decimals by 10, 100 or 1,000.

When you move down one row on a Gattegno chart, the number becomes **10 times smaller**. $0.3 \div 10 = 0.03$

When you move down two rows on a Gattegno chart, the number becomes **100 times smaller**.
$50 \div 100 = 0.5$ $0.7 \div 100 = 0.007$

100	200	300	400	500	600	700	800	900
10	20	30	40	50	60	70	80	90
1	2	3	4	5	6	7	8	9
0·1	0·2	0·3	0·4	0·5	0·6	0·7	0·8	0·9
0·01	0·02	0·03	0·04	0·05	0·06	0·07	0·08	0·09
0·001	0·002	0·003	0·004	0·005	0·006	0·007	0·008	0·009

When you move down three rows on a Gattegno chart, the number becomes **1,000 times smaller**. $9 \div 1,000 = 0.009$

Dividing by 10

When we **divide** a **whole number** or a **decimal** by 10, the value of each **digit** in the number becomes 10 times smaller and the digits move one **place value** to the right.

100s	10s	1s ·	$\frac{1}{10}$s
7	3	1 ·	
	7	3 ·	1

$731 \div 10 = 73.1$

100s	10s	1s ·	$\frac{1}{10}$s	$\frac{1}{100}$s	$\frac{1}{1,000}$s
3	4	1 ·	6	8	
	3	4 ·	1	6	8

$341.68 \div 10 = 34.168$

Include a zero as a **place holder**.

1s ·	$\frac{1}{10}$s	$\frac{1}{100}$s
7 ·	6	
0 ·	7	6

$7.6 \div 10 = 0.76$

1s ·	$\frac{1}{10}$s	$\frac{1}{100}$s	$\frac{1}{1,000}$s
5 ·	1	2	
0 ·	5	1	2

$5.12 \div 10 = 0.512$

$24.69 \div 10 = 2.469$

10	20	30	40	50	60	70	80	90
1	2	3	4	5	6	7	8	9
0·1	0·2	0·3	0·4	0·5	0·6	0·7	0·8	0·9
0·01	0·02	0·03	0·04	0·05	0·06	0·07	0·08	0·09
0·001	0·002	0·003	0·004	0·005	0·006	0·007	0·008	0·009

Dividing by 100

When we divide a whole number or a decimal by 100, the value of each digit in the number becomes 100 times smaller and the digits move two place values to the right.

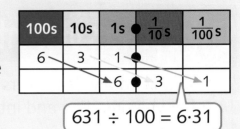

100s	10s	1s •	$\frac{1}{10}$ s	$\frac{1}{100}$ s
6	3	1		
		6 •	3	1

$631 \div 100 = 6 \cdot 31$

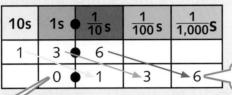

10s	1s •	$\frac{1}{10}$ s	$\frac{1}{100}$ s	$\frac{1}{1,000}$ s
1	3 •	6		
	0 •	1	3	6

$13 \cdot 6 \div 100 = 0 \cdot 136$

Include zeros as place holders

1s •	$\frac{1}{10}$ s	$\frac{1}{100}$ s	$\frac{1}{1,000}$ s
4 •	9		
0 •	0	4	9

$4 \cdot 9 \div 100 = 0 \cdot 049$

$357 \cdot 8 \div 100 = 3 \cdot 578$

100	200	300	400	500	600	700	800	900
10	20	30	40	50	60	70	80	90
1	2	3	4	5	6	7	8	9
0·1	0·2	0·3	0·4	0·5	0·6	0·7	0·8	0·9
0·01	0·02	0·03	0·04	0·05	0·06	0·07	0·08	0·09
0·001	0·002	0·003	0·004	0·005	0·006	0·007	0·008	0·009

Dividing by 1,000

When we divide a whole number or a decimal by 1,000, the value of each digit in the number becomes 1,000 times smaller and the digits move three place values to the right.

1s •	$\frac{1}{10}$ s	$\frac{1}{100}$ s	$\frac{1}{1,000}$ s
2 •			
0 •	0	0	2

$2 \div 1,000 = 0 \cdot 002$

10s	1s •	$\frac{1}{10}$ s	$\frac{1}{100}$ s	$\frac{1}{1,000}$ s
5	8 •			
	0 •	0	5	8

$58 \div 1,000 = 0 \cdot 058$

Include zeros as place holders.

$479 \div 1,000 = 0 \cdot 479$

100	200	300	400	500	600	700	800	900
10	20	30	40	50	60	70	80	90
1	2	3	4	5	6	7	8	9
0·1	0·2	0·3	0·4	0·5	0·6	0·7	0·8	0·9
0·01	0·02	0·03	0·04	0·05	0·06	0·07	0·08	0·09
0·001	0·002	0·003	0·004	0·005	0·006	0·007	0·008	0·009

What happens when you divide each of these decimals by 1,000?

| 0·3 | 7·4 | 2·35 | 418·67 |

Pages 80-81, 84-85, 92-93

Divide powers of 10 into 2, 4, 5 and 10 equal parts

Pages 60-61, 78-79

Being able to divide powers of 10 into 2, 4, 5 and 10 equal parts is useful when reading and interpreting measuring instruments and graph scales.

We know that: $10^2 = 10 \times 10 = 100$

The small 2 written above the 10 means 10 is **multiplied by itself** 2 times.

We call the small raised number the **exponent** or **index** or **power**. It tells us how many times to multiply a number by itself.

When the exponent is 2, a number is multiplied by itself 2 times.

We can say: < 10 to the power of 2 is equal to 100.

We can also say: < 10 **squared** is 100.

When the exponent is 3, a number is multiplied by itself 3 times.

So, $10^3 = 10 \times 10 \times 10 = 1,000$

We can say: < 10 to the power of 3 is equal to 1,000.

We can also say: < 10 **cubed** is 1,000.

These are the **powers of 10** from 10,000,000 to 1.

$10^7 = 10,000,000$	$10^6 = 1,000,000$	$10^5 = 100,000$	$10^4 = 10,000$
$10^3 = 1,000$	$10^2 = 100$	$10^1 = 10$	$10^0 = 1$

Look at these bar models and the models on page 81. What's the same about the models? What's different? What patterns do you notice?

10,000,000	
5,000,000	5,000,000

1,000,000	
500,000	500,000

100,000	
50,000	50,000

10,000	
5,000	5,000

1,000	
500	500

100	
50	50

In each of these bar models, the **whole** has been **divided into** 2 equal parts. To find the **value** of each part, the whole is **halved** or **divided by** 2.

10	
5	5

1	
0·5	0·5

In each of these bar models, the whole has been divided into 4 equal parts. To find the value of each part, the whole is divided by 4.

10,000,000			
2,500,000	2,500,000	2,500,000	2,500,000

100,000			
25,000	25,000	25,000	25,000

1,000			
250	250	250	250

10			
2·5	2·5	2·5	2·5

1,000,000			
250,000	250,000	250,000	250,000

10,000			
2,500	2,500	2,500	2,500

100			
25	25	25	25

1			
0·25	0·25	0·25	0·25

In each of these bar models, the whole has been divided into 5 equal parts. To find the value of each part, the whole is divided by 5.

10,000,000				
2,000,000	2,000,000	2,000,000	2,000,000	2,000,000

100,000				
20,000	20,000	20,000	20,000	20,000

1,000				
200	200	200	200	200

10				
2	2	2	2	2

1,000,000				
200,000	200,000	200,000	200,000	200,000

10,000				
2,000	2,000	2,000	2,000	2,000

100				
20	20	20	20	20

1				
0·2	0·2	0·2	0·2	0·2

In each of these bar models, the whole has been divided into 10 equal parts. To find the value of each part, the whole is divided by 10.

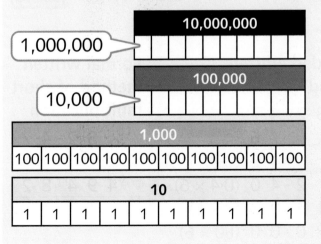

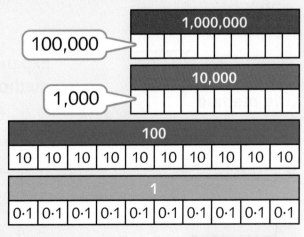

Pages 84-85

Decimals

Pages 30–33, 60–61, 64–65, 70–71, 76–77

Multiply a decimal by a whole number

We apply our understanding of place value, multiplication tables facts and multiplying whole numbers when we multiply decimals.

$7 \cdot 56 \times 8 = \boxed{60 \cdot 48}$

Grid method

×	7	0·5	0·06	
8	56	4	0·48	= 60·48

⚠ **ALWAYS:**
Estimate
Calculate
Check

Expanded written method

```
    7 · 5 6
  ×       8          leads to
    0 · 4 8   (0·06 × 8)
    4 · 0 0   (0·5 × 8)
  5 6 · 0 0   (7 × 8)
  6 0 · 4 8
  1
```

Formal written method of short multiplication

```
      7 · 5 6
  ×         8
    6 0 · 4 8
        4   4
```

We can also work out the answer to this calculation by converting the **decimal** to a **whole number** before calculating, then converting the **product** back to a decimal.

7·56 × 8 is **equivalent** to 756 × 8 ÷ 100

Expanded written method

```
    7 5 6
  ×     8          leads to
      4 8   (6 × 8)
    4 0 0   (50 × 8)
  5 6 0 0   (700 × 8)
  6 0 4 8
  1
```

Formal written method of short multiplication

```
      7 5 6
  ×       8
    6 0 4 8
      4   4
```

6,048 ÷ 100 = $\boxed{60·48}$

$82 \cdot 47 \times 6 = \boxed{494 \cdot 82}$

Grid method

×	80	2	0·4	0·07	
6	480	12	2·4	0·42	= 494·82

Expanded written method

```
    8 2 · 4 7
  ×         6          leads to
      0 · 4 2   (0·07 × 6)
      2 · 4 0   (0·4 × 6)
    1 2 · 0 0   (2 × 6)
  4 8 0 · 0 0   (80 × 6)
  4 9 4 · 8 2
```

Formal written method of short multiplication

```
    8 2 · 4 7
  ×         6
  4 9 4 · 8 2
    1   2   4
```

82·47 × 6 is equivalent to 8,247 × 6 ÷ 100

Expanded written method

```
    8 2 4 7
×         6
    4 2      (7 × 6)
    2 4 0    (40 × 6)
  1 2 0 0    (200 × 6)
4 8 0 0 0    (8,000 × 6)
4 9 4 8 2
```

leads to

Formal written method of short multiplication

```
    8 2 4 7
×         6
  4 9 4 8 2
    1 2 4
```

49,482 ÷ 100 = $\boxed{494\cdot82}$

Remember

```
    8 2 4 7
×   ₁ ₂ ₄ 6
  4 9 4 8 2
```

For short multiplication you can also write the regrouped values like this.

5·68 × 76 = $\boxed{431\cdot68}$

Grid method

×	5	0·6	0·08
70	350	42	5·6
6	30	3·6	0·48

397·6 + 34·08 = 431·68

Expanded written method

```
      5 · 6 8
×         7 6
      0 · 4 8    (0·08 × 6)
      3 · 6 0    (0·6 × 6)
    3 0 · 0 0    (5 × 6)
      5 · 6 0    (0·08 × 70)
    4 2 · 0 0    (0·6 × 70)
  3 5 0 · 0 0    (5 × 70)
  4 3 1 · 6 8
      1 1 1
```

leads to

Formal written method of long multiplication

```
      5 · 6 8
×         7 6
    3 4⁴· 0⁴ 8    (5·68 × 6)
    3 9⁴ 7⁵· 6 0  (5·68 × 70)
    4 3 1 · 6 8
        1 1
```

5·68 × 76 is equivalent to 568 × 76 ÷ 100

Expanded written method

```
      5 6 8
×       7 6
        4 8    (8 × 6)
      3 6 0    (60 × 6)
    3 0 0 0    (500 × 6)
      5 6 0    (8 × 70)
    4 2 0 0    (60 × 70)
  3 5 0 0 0    (500 × 70)
  4 3 1 6 8
      1 1 1
```

leads to

Formal written method of long multiplication

```
      5 6 8
×       7 6
    3 4⁴ 0⁴ 8    (568 × 6)
    3 9⁴ 7⁵ 6 0  (568 × 70)
    4 3 1 6 8
        1 1
```

43,168 ÷ 100 = $\boxed{431\cdot68}$

Divide a decimal by a whole number

Pages 34-37,
60-61, 64-65,
70-71, 78-81

We apply our understanding of place value, multiplication and division facts, and dividing whole numbers when we divide decimals.

$4.71 \div 3 = \boxed{1.57}$

⚠️ **ALWAYS:**

Estimate   **C**alculate   **C**heck

Regrouping

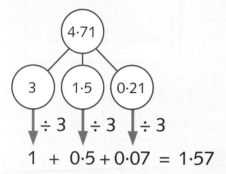

$$1 + 0.5 + 0.07 = 1.57$$

Expanded written method

$$
\begin{array}{r}
1 \cdot 5\ 7 \\
3\overline{)4 \cdot 7\ 1} \\
-\ 3 \cdot 0\ 0 \quad (1 \times 3) \\
\hline
1 \cdot 7\ 1 \\
-\ 1 \cdot 5\ 0 \quad (0.5 \times 3) \\
\hline
0 \cdot 2\ 1 \\
-\ 0 \cdot 2\ 1 \quad (0.07 \times 3) \\
\hline
0 \cdot 0\ 0
\end{array}
$$

leads to

Formal written method of short division

$$
\begin{array}{r}
1 \cdot 5\ 7 \\
3\overline{)4 \cdot {}^17\ {}^21}
\end{array}
$$

We can also work out the answer to this calculation by converting the **decimal** to a **whole number** before calculating, then converting the **quotient** back to a decimal.

$4.71 \div 3$ is **equivalent** to $471 \div 3 \div 100$

Expanded written method

$$
\begin{array}{r}
1\ 5\ 7 \\
3\overline{)4\ 7\ 1} \\
-\ 3\ 0\ 0 \quad (100 \times 3) \\
\hline
1\ 7\ 1 \\
-\ 1\ 5\ 0 \quad (50 \times 3) \\
\hline
2\ 1 \\
-\quad 2\ 1 \quad (7 \times 3) \\
\hline
0\ 0
\end{array}
$$

leads to

Formal written method of short division

$$
\begin{array}{r}
1\ 5\ 7 \\
3\overline{)4\ {}^17\ {}^21}
\end{array}
$$

$157 \div 100 = \boxed{1.57}$

$51.45 \div 7 = \boxed{7.35}$

Regrouping

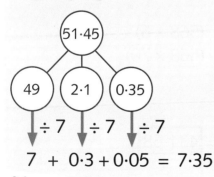

$$7 + 0.3 + 0.05 = 7.35$$

Expanded written method

$$
\begin{array}{r}
7 \cdot 3\ 5 \\
7\overline{){}^45\ {}^11 \cdot 4\ 5} \\
-\ 4\ 9 \cdot 0\ 0 \quad (7 \times 7) \\
\hline
0\ 2 \cdot 4\ 5 \\
-\ 0\ 2 \cdot 1\ 0 \quad (0.3 \times 7) \\
\hline
0\ 0 \cdot 3\ 5 \\
-\ 0\ 0 \cdot 3\ 5 \quad (0.05 \times 7) \\
\hline
0\ 0 \cdot 0\ 0
\end{array}
$$

leads to

Formal written method of short division

$$
\begin{array}{r}
7 \cdot 3\ 5 \\
7\overline{)5\ {}^51 \cdot {}^24\ {}^35}
\end{array}
$$

$51·45 \div 7$ is equivalent to $5{,}145 \div 7 \div 100$

Expanded written method

leads to

Formal written method of short division

```
        7 3 5
7)⁴5¹1 4 5
 − 4 9 0 0   (700 × 7)
   2 4 5
 −   2 1 0   (30 × 7)
     3 5
 −     3 5   (5 × 7)
     0 0
```

```
        7 3 5
7)5 ⁵1 ²4 ³5
```

$735 \div 100 = \boxed{7·35}$

$45·64 \div 14 = \boxed{3·26}$

Expanded written method

leads to

Formal written method of long division

```
        3 · 2 6
1 4)4 5 · 6 4
 − 4 2 · 0 0   (3 × 14)
   0 ²3 ·¹6 4
 − 0 2 · 8 0   (0·2 × 14)
   0 0 · 8 4
 − 0 0 · 8 4   (0·06 × 14)
   0 0 · 0 0
```

```
        3 · 2 6
1 4)4 5 · 6 4
 − 4 2 · ↓
   ²3 ·¹6 ↓
 −   2 · 8 ↓
     0 · 8 4
 −   0 · 8 4
     0 · 0 0
```

$45·64 \div 14$ is equivalent to $4{,}564 \div 14 \div 100$

Expanded written method

leads to

Formal written method of long division

```
        3 2 6
1 4)4 5 6 4
 − 4 2 0 0   (300 × 14)
   ²3¹6 4
 −   2 8 0   (20 × 14)
     8 4
 −     8 4   (6 × 14)
     0 0
```

```
        3 2 6
1 4)4 5 6 4
 − 4 2 ↓
   ²3¹6 ↓
 −   2 8 ↓
     8 4
 −     8 4
     0 0
```

$326 \div 100 = \boxed{3·26}$

Fractions to decimals

Pages 24-25, 34-37, 42-43, 60-61

A fraction can be thought of as a division of the numerator by the denominator.

numerator

$\frac{3}{4}$ — division bar or vinculum

denominator

Each square is 1 out of 100 equal squares. This square is 1 hundredth. As a fraction, we write this as $\frac{1}{100}$. As a decimal, we write this as 0·01.

 Remember

Each row (or column) is 1 out of 10 equal rows (or columns). This row is 1 tenth. As a fraction, we write this as $\frac{1}{10}$. As a decimal, we write this as 0·1.

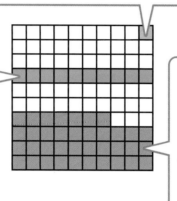

There are 37 green squares. So, 37 hundredths are shaded green. As a fraction, we write this as $\frac{37}{100}$. As a decimal, we write this as 0·37.

$\frac{3}{4} \rightarrow 0.75$ — What's the same? What's different?

To convert a fraction to a decimal, use equivalent fractions to make the denominator 10, 100 or 1,000.

$$\frac{3}{4} \overset{\times 25}{=} \frac{75}{100} = 0.75 \quad \underset{\times 25}{}$$

Look at these fractions and equivalent decimals.

$$\frac{2}{5} \overset{\times 2}{\underset{\times 2}{=}} \frac{4}{10} = 0.4 \qquad \frac{3}{50} \overset{\times 2}{\underset{\times 2}{=}} \frac{6}{100} = 0.06 \qquad \frac{7}{20} \overset{\times 5}{\underset{\times 5}{=}} \frac{35}{100} = 0.35$$

$$\frac{74}{250} \overset{\times 4}{\underset{\times 4}{=}} \frac{296}{1,000} = 0.296 \qquad \frac{258}{3,000} \overset{\div 3}{\underset{\div 3}{=}} \frac{86}{1,000} = 0.086$$

Sometimes there is more than one way to convert a fraction to an equivalent decimal.

Look at this example.

$$\frac{13}{100} \xrightarrow[\div 5]{\div 5} \frac{65}{500} \xrightarrow[\times 2]{\times 2} \frac{130}{1{,}000} = 0.13$$

It's easy to convert a fraction to an equivalent decimal when the denominator is a **factor** or **multiple** of a **power of 10**.

Powers of 10 are 10, 100, 1,000, and so on.

Remember

Look at this fraction: $\frac{7}{8}$

To convert this fraction to an equivalent decimal, we can use **short division** to **divide** the **numerator** by the denominator.

$\frac{7}{8} = 7 \div 8$

$$8 \overline{)7 .{}^{7}0\,{}^{6}0\,{}^{4}0} \quad \begin{array}{c} 0 . 8\ 7\ 5 \end{array}$$

$7 \div 8$ **is equal to** 0.875.

So, $\frac{7}{8}$ is equal to 0.875.

We can use this method to convert any fraction to an equivalent decimal. This includes fractions whose denominator is a factor or multiple of a power of 10, and improper fractions.

$\frac{3}{25} = 3 \div 25$

$$25 \overline{)3 .{}^{3}0\,{}^{5}0} \quad \begin{array}{c} 0 . 1\ 2 \end{array}$$

$3 \div 25$ is equal to 0.12.

So, $\frac{3}{25}$ is equal to 0.12.

$\frac{8}{5} = 8 \div 5$

$$5 \overline{)8 .{}^{3}0} \quad \begin{array}{c} 1 . 6 \end{array}$$

$8 \div 5$ is equal to 1.6.

So, $\frac{8}{5}$ is equal to 1.6.

  Use your preferred method to convert these fractions to decimals.

| $\frac{9}{20}$ | $\frac{83}{250}$ | $\frac{5}{8}$ | $\frac{114}{2{,}000}$ | $\frac{5}{4}$ | $\frac{4}{5}$ |

Pages 90–91

Percentages

Pages 60-63

Per cent means per hundred. It represents the number of parts in every 100.

Percentages are like fractions. They tell us the number of parts in every hundred or the number of parts per hundred.

The sign for per cent is %.

We see percentages in everyday life, including on packaged food.

Each ½ pack serving contains				
MED	LOW	MED	HIGH	MED
Calories	Sugar	Fat	Sat Fat	Salt
353	0·9g	20·3g	10·8g	1·1g
19%	1%	29%	54%	18%
of your recommended daily amount				

This label tells us that half of this packet of food contains 18% of the recommended daily amount of salt.

The label tells us that half of this packet of food contains only 1% of the recommended daily amount of sugar, but 54% of the recommended daily amount of saturated fats.

Like with numbers, we can compare and order percentages.

1% < 18% < 19% < 29% < 54%

A percentage is an amount out of 100.

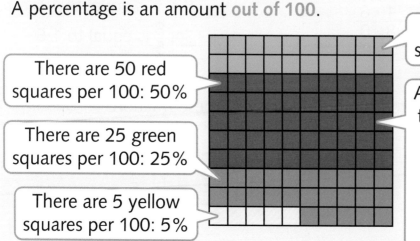

There are 20 blue squares per 100: 20%

There are 50 red squares per 100: 50%

There are 25 green squares per 100: 25%

There are 5 yellow squares per 100: 5%

All the squares added together – blue, red, green and yellow – represent 100%. 100% is the whole amount. 100% is equal to 1.

The square at the bottom of page 88 is divided into 100 equal parts. We can find a percentage of any total amount, not just 100.

Look at this bar model.
What per cent of the model is shaded blue?

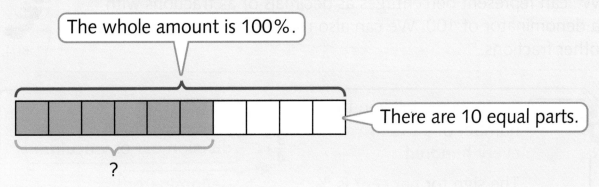

The whole amount is 100%.

There are 10 equal parts.

?

To find the percentage represented by one part, we **divide** 100 by the number of parts.

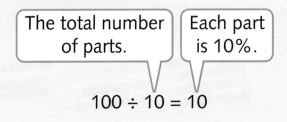

The total number of parts.

Each part is 10%.

$100 \div 10 = 10$

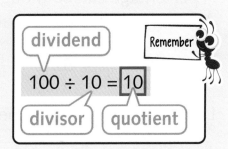

Remember

dividend

$100 \div 10 = \boxed{10}$

divisor   quotient

To find what percentage of the model is shaded blue, we **multiply** the quotient (10) by the number of shaded parts (6).

$10 \times 6 = 60$

So, 60% of the model is shaded blue.

What per cent of each shape is shaded?

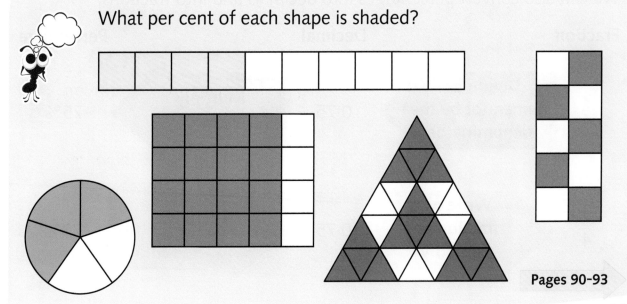

Pages 90-93

Equivalences

Pages 40-45, 60-63, 88-89

We can represent percentages as decimals or as fractions with a denominator of 100. We can also use percentages to express other fractions.

 Remember **Percentages** tell you the number of **parts in every hundred**.

The sign for **per cent** is %.

$\frac{3}{4}$ — numerator
— division bar or vinculum
— denominator

A percentage can be thought of as another name for hundredths. A fraction expressed as a hundredth can also be expressed as a percentage.

$\frac{1}{100} = 1\%$ $\frac{32}{100} = 32\%$ $\frac{83}{100} = 83\%$

Look at this group of 10 pencils:

$\frac{6}{10}$ of these pencils are blue. This is the same as $\frac{60}{100}$.
So, you can say that 60% of these pencils are blue.

Fractions, decimals and percentages can have equivalent values.

We can convert fractions into decimals and into percentages.
We can also convert percentages into decimals and into fractions.

Fraction	Decimal	Percentage

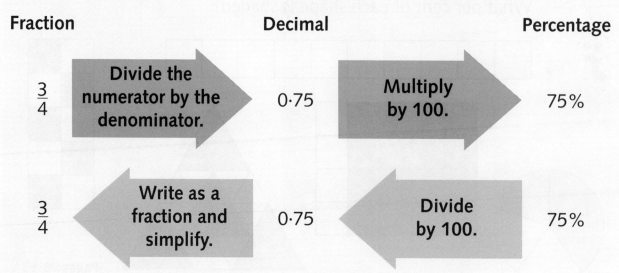

$\frac{3}{4}$	**Divide the numerator by the denominator.** → 0·75	**Multiply by 100.** → 75%
$\frac{3}{4}$	← **Write as a fraction and simplify.** 0·75	← **Divide by 100.** 75%

The table below shows different ways to represent and write the same fraction.

Part of a whole	Part of a group	Fraction	Decimal	Percentage
		$\frac{1}{20}$	0·05	5%
		$\frac{1}{10}$	0·1	10%
		$\frac{1}{5}$	0·2	20%
		$\frac{1}{4}$	0·25	25%
		$\frac{3}{10}$	0·3	30%
		$\frac{2}{5}$	0·4	40%
		$\frac{1}{2}$	0·5	50%
		$\frac{3}{5}$	0·6	60%
		$\frac{7}{10}$	0·7	70%
		$\frac{3}{4}$	0·75	75%
		$\frac{4}{5}$	0·8	80%
		$\frac{9}{10}$	0·9	90%

Look at the list of fractions. Can you identify any fractions that are equivalent to these?

We can use equivalences to compare and order fractions, decimals and percentages.

$$0.4 \; > \; 5\% \qquad\qquad \frac{3}{5} \; > \; 0.3 \qquad\qquad \frac{1}{4} \; < \; 50\%$$

$$5\% \; < \; \frac{1}{4} \; < \; 0.3 \; < \; 0.4 \; < \; 50\% \; < \; \frac{3}{5}$$

Write

Choose different pairs of fractions, decimals and percentages and compare them using the inequalities symbols.

| 0·35 | 40% | $\frac{8}{50}$ | 0·67 | $\frac{24}{100}$ | 55% |

Now write all six fractions, decimals and percentages in descending order.

Pages 92-93

Percentages

Calculate a percentage of an amount

Pages 28-29, 60-61, 78-79, 88-91

We can find a percentage of any total amount. The total can be a number or a quantity. We can use different methods to find percentages, including applying our understanding of fractional equivalences.

 To calculate **unit** fractions of an amount:

1. Find the total amount – the **whole**.

2. **Divide** the whole by the denominator.

$\frac{1}{2}$ — numerator — division bar or vinculum — denominator

Let's look at these **percentage** and **fraction equivalences**.

50% is equivalent to $\frac{1}{2}$.

To find 50% of an amount, divide by 2.

50% of 118 = 59

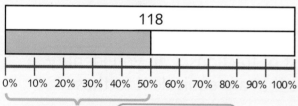

? — 118 ÷ 2 = 59

25% is equivalent to $\frac{1}{4}$.

To find 25% of an amount, divide by 4.

25% of 268 = 67

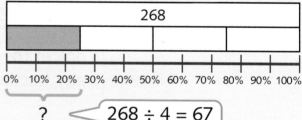

? — 268 ÷ 4 = 67

10% is equivalent to $\frac{1}{10}$.

To find 10% of an amount, divide by 10.

10% of 400 = 40

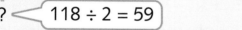

? — 400 ÷ 10 = 40

1% is equivalent to $\frac{1}{100}$.

To find 1% of an amount, divide by 100.

1% of 400 = 4

400 ÷ 100 = 4

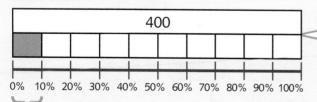

We can apply our knowledge of finding 50%, 25%, 10% and 1% of amounts to finding other percentages of amounts.

We can use different methods to work out percentages.

20% of 290 = 58

To calculate 20%:

Find 20% by dividing by 10, then multiplying by 2.

$$10\% \text{ of } 290 = 290 \div 10$$
$$= 29$$
$$20\% \text{ of } 290 = 2 \times 29$$
$$= 58$$

OR

20% is equivalent to $\frac{1}{5}$, so divide by 5.

$$20\% \text{ of } 290 = 290 \div 5$$
$$= 58$$

65% of 420 = 273

To calculate 65%:

Find 60% by dividing by 10, then multiplying by 6. Find 5% by calculating half of 10%. Add 60% and 5% to find 65%.

$$10\% \text{ of } 420 = 420 \div 10$$
$$= 42$$
$$60\% \text{ of } 420 = 6 \times 42$$
$$= 252$$
$$5\% \text{ of } 420 = 42 \div 2$$
$$= 21$$
$$252 + 21 = 273$$

OR

Find 70% by dividing by 10, then multiplying by 7. Find 5% by calculating half of 10%. Subtract 5% from 70% to find 65%.

How else could you work out 65% of 420?

$$10\% \text{ of } 420 = 420 \div 10$$
$$= 42$$
$$70\% \text{ of } 420 = 7 \times 42$$
$$= 294$$
$$5\% \text{ of } 420 = 42 \div 2$$
$$= 21$$
$$294 - 21 = 273$$

 Write

Use your preferred method to calculate:

40% of 175 = ☐   35% of 280 = ☐

6% of 4,100 = ☐   52% of 5,400 = ☐

 Say

Compare your answers to the calculations above, and the methods you used, with a partner.

Which methods were the most effective and efficient?

Year 6 Number facts

Tenths and hundredths addition and subtraction facts

If you know that 8 + 6 = 14, you can use this to work out facts such as:

0·8 + 0·6 = 1·4

and

0·08 + 0·06 = 0·14

Addition can be done in any order. So,

0·8 + 0·6 = 1·4

and

0·6 + 0·8 = 1·4

Addition is the inverse of subtraction. So, if you know that

0·8 + 0·6 = 1·4

you also know that

1·4 − 0·6 = 0·8

and

1·4 − 0·8 = 0·6

+	0	0·1	0·2	0·3	0·4	0·5	0·6	0·7	0·8	0·9	1
0	0	0·1	0·2	0·3	0·4	0·5	0·6	0·7	0·8	0·9	1
0·1	0·1	0·2	0·3	0·4	0·5	0·6	0·7	0·8	0·9	1	1·1
0·2	0·2	0·3	0·4	0·5	0·6	0·7	0·8	0·9	1	1·1	1·2
0·3	0·3	0·4	0·5	0·6	0·7	0·8	0·9	1	1·1	1·2	1·3
0·4	0·4	0·5	0·6	0·7	0·8	0·9	1	1·1	1·2	1·3	1·4
0·5	0·5	0·6	0·7	0·8	0·9	1	1·1	1·2	1·3	1·4	1·5
0·6	0·6	0·7	0·8	0·9	1	1·1	1·2	1·3	1·4	1·5	1·6
0·7	0·7	0·8	0·9	1	1·1	1·2	1·3	1·4	1·5	1·6	1·7
0·8	0·8	0·9	1	1·1	1·2	1·3	1·4	1·5	1·6	1·7	1·8
0·9	0·9	1	1·1	1·2	1·3	1·4	1·5	1·6	1·7	1·8	1·9
1	1	1·1	1·2	1·3	1·4	1·5	1·6	1·7	1·8	1·9	2

+	0	0·01	0·02	0·03	0·04	0·05	0·06	0·07	0·08	0·09	0·1
0	0	0·01	0·02	0·03	0·04	0·05	0·06	0·07	0·08	0·09	0·1
0·01	0·01	0·02	0·03	0·04	0·05	0·06	0·07	0·08	0·09	0·1	0·11
0·02	0·02	0·03	0·04	0·05	0·06	0·07	0·08	0·09	0·1	0·11	0·12
0·03	0·03	0·04	0·05	0·06	0·07	0·08	0·09	0·1	0·11	0·12	0·13
0·04	0·04	0·05	0·06	0·07	0·08	0·09	0·1	0·11	0·12	0·13	0·14
0·05	0·05	0·06	0·07	0·08	0·09	0·1	0·11	0·12	0·13	0·14	0·15
0·06	0·06	0·07	0·08	0·09	0·1	0·11	0·12	0·13	0·14	0·15	0·16
0·07	0·07	0·08	0·09	0·1	0·11	0·12	0·13	0·14	0·15	0·16	0·17
0·08	0·08	0·09	0·1	0·11	0·12	0·13	0·14	0·15	0·16	0·17	0·18
0·09	0·09	0·1	0·11	0·12	0·13	0·14	0·15	0·16	0·17	0·18	0·19
0·1	0·1	0·11	0·12	0·13	0·14	0·15	0·16	0·17	0·18	0·19	0·2

Multiplication and division facts

Multiplication can be done in any order.

So, 3 × 4 = 12 and

4 × 3 = 12

Multiplication is the inverse of division.

So, if you know that 3 × 4 = 12 you also know that

12 ÷ 4 = 3 and 12 ÷ 3 = 4

×	1	2	3	4	5	6	7	8	9	10	11	12
1	1	2	3	4	5	6	7	8	9	10	11	12
2	2	4	6	8	10	12	14	16	18	20	22	24
3	3	6	9	12	15	18	21	24	27	30	33	36
4	4	8	12	16	20	24	28	32	36	40	44	48
5	5	10	15	20	25	30	35	40	45	50	55	60
6	6	12	18	24	30	36	42	48	54	60	66	72
7	7	14	21	28	35	42	49	56	63	70	77	84
8	8	16	24	32	40	48	56	64	72	80	88	96
9	9	18	27	36	45	54	63	72	81	90	99	108
10	10	20	30	40	50	60	70	80	90	100	110	120
11	11	22	33	44	55	66	77	88	99	110	121	132
12	12	24	36	48	60	72	84	96	108	120	132	144

Tenths and hundredths multiplication and division facts

If you know that

$3 \times 4 = 12$

you can use this to work out facts such as:

$0.3 \times 4 = 1.2$

and

$0.03 \times 4 = 0.12$

Multiplication is the inverse of division. So, if you know that

$0.3 \times 4 = 1.2$

you also know that

$1.2 \div 4 = 0.3$

and

$0.12 \div 4 = 0.03$

×	0.1	0.2	0.3	0.4	0.5	0.6	0.7	0.8	0.9	1	1.1	1.2
1	0.1	0.2	0.3	0.4	0.5	0.6	0.7	0.8	0.9	1	1.1	1.2
2	0.2	0.4	0.6	0.8	1	1.2	1.4	1.6	1.8	2	2.2	2.4
3	0.3	0.6	0.9	1.2	1.5	1.8	2.1	2.4	2.7	3	3.3	3.6
4	0.4	0.8	1.2	1.6	2	2.4	2.8	3.2	3.6	4	4.4	4.8
5	0.5	1	1.5	2	2.5	3	3.5	4	4.5	5	5.5	6
6	0.6	1.2	1.8	2.4	3	3.6	4.2	4.8	5.4	6	6.6	7.2
7	0.7	1.4	2.1	2.8	3.5	4.2	4.9	5.6	6.3	7	7.7	8.4
8	0.8	1.6	2.4	3.2	4	4.8	5.6	6.4	7.2	8	8.8	9.6
9	0.9	1.8	2.7	3.6	4.5	5.4	6.3	7.2	8.1	9	9.9	10.8
10	1	2	3	4	5	6	7	8	9	10	11	12
11	1.1	2.2	3.3	4.4	5.5	6.6	7.7	8.8	9.9	11	12.1	13.2
12	1.2	2.4	3.6	4.8	6	7.2	8.4	9.6	10.8	12	13.2	14.4

×	0.01	0.02	0.03	0.04	0.05	0.06	0.07	0.08	0.09	0.1	0.11	0.12
1	0.01	0.02	0.03	0.04	0.05	0.06	0.07	0.08	0.09	0.1	0.11	0.12
2	0.02	0.04	0.06	0.08	0.1	0.12	0.14	0.16	0.18	0.2	0.22	0.24
3	0.03	0.06	0.09	0.12	0.15	0.18	0.21	0.24	0.27	0.3	0.33	0.36
4	0.04	0.08	0.12	0.16	0.2	0.24	0.28	0.32	0.36	0.4	0.44	0.48
5	0.05	0.1	0.15	0.2	0.25	0.3	0.35	0.4	0.45	0.5	0.55	0.6
6	0.06	0.12	0.18	0.24	0.3	0.36	0.42	0.48	0.54	0.6	0.66	0.72
7	0.07	0.14	0.21	0.28	0.35	0.42	0.49	0.56	0.63	0.7	0.77	0.84
8	0.08	0.16	0.24	0.32	0.4	0.48	0.56	0.64	0.72	0.8	0.88	0.96
9	0.09	0.18	0.27	0.36	0.45	0.54	0.63	0.72	0.81	0.9	0.99	1.08
10	0.1	0.2	0.3	0.4	0.5	0.6	0.7	0.8	0.9	1	1.1	1.2
11	0.11	0.22	0.33	0.44	0.55	0.66	0.77	0.88	0.99	1.1	1.21	1.32
12	0.12	0.24	0.36	0.48	0.6	0.72	0.84	0.96	1.08	1.2	1.32	1.44